The Lugano Report

**On Preserving Capitalism
in the Twenty-first Century**

**With an Annexe and Afterword
by Susan George**

Pluto  **Press**

LONDON • STERLING, VIRGINIA

First published 1999 by Pluto Press
345 Archway Road, London N6 5AA
and 22883 Quicksilver Drive, Sterling, VA 20166–2012, USA

British Library Cataloguing in Publication Data
A catalogue record for this book is available from the British
Library

ISBN 0 7453 1537 2 hbk
ISBN 0 7453 1532 1 pbk

Library of Congress Cataloging-in-Publication Data
George, Susan.
    The Lugano report : on preserving capitalism in the twenty-first
century / with an annexe and afterword by Susan George.
        p.   cm.
    ISBN 0 7453 1537 2 (hbk)
    1. Free enterprise. 2. Capitalism. 3. Economic forecasting.
    I. Title
    HB95.G446 1999
    3330.12'2—dc21   99–12828
                                                              CIP

09   08   07   06   05   04   03   02   01
10   9   8   7   6   5   4   3   2

Designed and produced for Pluto Press by
Chase Publishing Services
Typeset from disk by Gawcott Typesetting
Printed in the European Union by Antony Rowe,
Chippenham, England

Contents

FROM: THE COMMISSIONING PARTIES

TO: THE WORKING PARTY

15 October 1996

Gentlemen,

We thank you for your gracious acceptance of our commission.

As you have already been informed, this work will require your nearly undivided attention and energies for the coming year. We shall expect your Report by the end of November 1997.

This Report is to be for the eyes of the Commissioners alone, its contents and the commission itself are not to be discussed or alluded to beyond the group and we expect you to exercise due regard for confidentiality in your dealings and communications with each other.

Your work should provide us with guidance in order to maintain, develop and deepen the scope of the liberal, free-market economy, and the process best summed up as 'globalisation'. You may be sure that your recommendations, which should be frank and forthright, will be acted upon. At our discretion, your conclusions may be shared with selected heads of state and their national security agencies as well as with leaders of the corporate and financial world.

Mr 'Gentian', who has already contacted each of you individually, will continue to act as our liaison person. He will see to practical matters, provide you with more detailed terms of reference and answer any questions you may have, save that of our several and collective identities.

We are certain that the interdisciplinary nature of your group, the calibre of your individual attainments and the firm personal commitment each of you brings to this vital work will result in a document of outstanding intellectual and practical relevance.

We wish you well.

Letter of Transmittal

28 November 1997

TO: THE COMMISSIONING PARTIES

Attached please find the Report of the Working Party which you designated to consider the future of the global economy and the free-market system. Our work was accomplished within the year allotted, between November 1996 and November 1997.

Although it may not be our place to do so, we wish to offer a tribute to the Commissioning Parties. The year over which we convened was in Dickensian terms 'the best of times and the worst of times'. It witnessed remarkable economic expansion and market euphoria but also intimations of crisis and emergency. Never before, perhaps, had the benefits of globalisation spread so rapidly to so many; never before had its dangers been so clear.

Our sponsors nonetheless chose to look beyond both the auspicious signs and the warning signals. They asked for impartiality and instructed us to reject received wisdom, to spare no feelings and to state our findings 'without fear or favour'. Such freedom is at once rare and burdensome. We hope to have borne this burden honourably.

According to our terms of reference, this Report is to remain confidential, an assurance which has allowed us to proceed with utmost frankness. The Working Party members are themselves personally bound and determined to maintain that confidentiality. Should the contents of this Report or the identities of its authors be divulged, in whole or in part, we will, singly and collectively, deny any connection with it and dispute its authenticity.

This is not to disavow our work; on the contrary and modesty aside, we believe that no other group, by whomever constituted, has come close to identifying the stark realities we confront today. We doubt, however, that the readers other than those for whom this Report is specifically intended would assimilate its contents with the requisite detachment and without strong emotional reactions colouring their perceptions. We consider the contents too important to run such a risk.

The Report is unanimously transmitted. This unanimity was not, however, readily arrived at. In the later stages of the process particularly, certain Working Party members voiced reservations concerning the implications of the arguments and recommendations made hereunder. However, as we progressed from diagnosis of the current state of the world to consideration of feasible alternative strategies and solutions, we became convinced that our recommendations constitute the only possible course of action. They derive, in fact, from principles, including moral principles, to which future generations, if not our own, can only adhere.

As to the aforementioned 'readers for whom the Report is specifically intended', we admit to some misgivings; we would have preferred to know more concerning the identities of the commissioners and the precise status of this document, even though we have been assured that our Report will be taken seriously by persons in a position to carry out some or all of its recommendations. Encouraged by this pledge, we have completed it to the best of our abilities and to our own satisfaction, regardless of its destination.

Our Report is as succinct as its vast subject matter allows but we have not provided a conventional 'Executive Summary'. We would have found such a procedure insulting to a readership which has invested substantial resources in the production of this document. We conclude that they will spare the time to read it in full.

We wish to thank our facilitator, Mr 'Gentian', for his admirable efficiency and for providing us with every convenience and comfort as our work has progresses over the past year. Our plenary sessions took place in the delightful Swiss lakeside town of Lugano; this is why, for us, it will remain *The Lugano Report*. Its more formal title is *On Preserving Capitalism in the Twenty-first Century*.

In keeping with the precautions taken during its elaboration, we will sign this Letter of Transmittal with our Working Party pseudonyms to which, if truth be told, we have become rather attached.

Signed: ASPHODEL, BURDOCK, CINQUEFOIL, DILL, EDEL-WEISS, FOXGLOVE, HAWKWEED, PENNYCRESS, SNOWBELL

Part One

1.1

Dangers

To our knowledge, no previous Working Party has been confronted with terms of reference at once as broad and as daunting as ours. We are asked:

- To identify the threats to the free-market capitalist system and the obstacles to its generalisation and preservation as we enter the new millennium.

- To examine the present course of the world economy in the light of those threats and obstacles.

- To recommend strategies, concrete measures and changes of direction maximising the probability that the free-market, globalised capitalist system will prevail.[1]

We shall consider the threats and dangers in the first part of this Report and proposals and recommendations in the second.

The group unreservedly shares the premise of the Commissioning Parties: a liberal, market-based, globalised world system should not merely remain the norm but triumph in the twenty-first century. We see an economic system based on individual freedom and risk as the guarantor of other freedoms and values.

We also accept the Commissioning Parties' challenge to dispense as far as possible with sentiment, prejudice and preconceptions in the elaboration of this Report. We hope and trust that our academic and cultural backgrounds suit us well to doing so.

Threats and Obstacles

Threats and obstacles to the liberal vision are pervasive and the system is in much greater danger than is commonly supposed. Protecting it in the coming century and beyond will be easier said than done!

Lest we be misunderstood, we do not foresee the renaissance of some neo-Soviet empire; we seriously doubt that any alternative world political–economic system can reasonably compete with the global market economy on theoretical or on practical grounds in the decades to come. A resurgent, credible Marxism or other alternative system is not on the cards. Nor do we believe that any religious dogma is likely to gain significant political or economic ascendancy, however peripherally troublesome it might be.

The threats to the system are more subtle than any posed by politics, ideology or faith. It is not enough that this system display substantial practical advantages and genuine theoretical coherence. No one can deny that millions presently profit from it, whether in its traditional North American and European strongholds or in the huge areas of the world more recently opened to its benefits.

Millions more fervently believe that they, too, can improve their lot; for capitalism is not merely an economic doctrine and an intellectual achievement but also a revolutionary, millennial force and a source of hope, just as communism once was. This, at the deepest level, is why they were deadly rivals.

The aspiration to material well-being in the here-and-now has proved far more powerful (not to mention more truthful) than the promises of communism or of religion, which defer gratification to some radiant, indeterminate future or to the afterlife. In such contests, the noise and clangour of the marketplace will always win out over the earthly or heavenly choirs of paradise postponed. Why, then, should the market system be threatened? We propose several reasons.

Potentially Catastrophic Ecological Breakdown

The danger signs are spread all around us yet scarcely register in the standard economic models. *Nature* is the greatest obstacle of all to the future of the free-market system and cannot be treated as an adversary. The message must be: protect or perish.

Whether or not professional economists are truly blind to ecological danger, they behave as if the less said about it the better. Perhaps they fear that revealing or analysing this major contradiction of our economic system would be detrimental to its preservation while undermining the scientific pretensions of their discipline and the standing of their own profession.

Whatever the limitations and mass denial of mainstream economics, it has become clear since the path-breaking work of Nicholas Georgescu-Roegen[2] in the early 1970s (subsequently popularised by Professor Herman Daly and others) that economies must ultimately be analysed in terms of actual or potential energy flows and 'entropy', or 'used up', non-available energy. In other words, the economy, like other physical systems (including the human body) must be understood within the framework of the Second Law of Thermodynamics.[3]

This law applies for the simple reason that our economic system is a sub-system of the natural world and does not encompass that world. To consider the economy as the encompassing system and nature as a mere sub-system and then to examine economic phenomena using a 'mechanistic episte-mology' (Georgescu-Roegen's term) is a purely artificial construct. We believe it is also a recipe for disaster.

In mechanics, all phenomena are reversible. Reversibility is similarly assumed by nearly all neo-classical, Keynesian and Marxist economists. No event, so to speak, leaves a durable mark; everything, given time, may revert to 'initial conditions'. As Georgescu-Roegen makes clear, this is nonsense:

> The economic process is not an isolated, self-sustaining process. This process cannot go on without a continuous exchange which alters the environment in a cumulative way and without being, in its turn, influenced by these alterations.

Recognising this basic truth would involve recasting much of the academic canon as presently handed down from one gener-ation to the next, a task which occasions limited theoretical and practical enthusiasm.

Our duty, however, is not to shield any profession but to describe the world as it is. To deny the enormous pressures placed upon nature by capitalist economies (and even more by formerly socialist ones) is foolish. Standard economic calcula-tions treat the consumption of both renewable and non-renewable resources ('natural capital') as income and as contributions to growth. Growth, in turn, is considered synonymous with economic well-being.

In such a system, a forest razed and sold for logs, sawn timber, charcoal, furniture, and so on is counted only on the positive side of the ledger. The destruction of the natural capital represented by that forest and the 'services' it provides, such as its capacity to absorb CO_2, to stabilise the soil, to shelter species diversity, are nowhere to be found.

Air, water and soil are counted as free, or nearly free, goods; their scarcity value is not recognised or calculated. Depletion of fish stocks, topsoil, minerals, the ozone shield, wildlife species, rare plants, and so on is either regarded as income or compensated by subsidies to the very producers intent on further depletion (such as agribusiness and natural resource companies).

For the longer-term success of liberalism, such an attitude is suicidal. The economy is contained in the finite, physical world, not vice versa. The reality of the biosphere is a 'given'; its resources cannot be expanded; its absorptive capacity cannot be increased by human intervention; once damaged it does not revert to 'initial conditions', or only in Keynes' 'long run in which we are all dead'.

The economy, rather, transforms inputs of energy and materials into outputs of goods and services, disposing of the wastes, pollution and heat (entropy) engendered by this process into the biosphere. In other words, the economy is an *open system operating within a closed one.*

Present descriptive, computing and accounting techniques do not tell us what we need to know. They are inadequate tools because corporate and national accounts are 'mathematical–mechanical' constructions and assume an economy operating independently from nature.

Goods and services extracted from the biosphere are thus undervalued or not valued at all; pollution, waste and heat returned to the biosphere are not measured as costs. Real ecological costs are 'externalised' and as such must be borne by society and the planet as a whole.

Questions of *scale* therefore immediately arise. If the scale of the economy is small with regard to the biosphere, as it was until this century, environmental questions are not pertinent, much less paramount, or only occasionally and locally. As the economy grows, however, scale becomes critical.

The world now produces in less than two weeks the equivalent of the entire physical output of the year 1900. Economic output (or 'throughput', which conveys a more dynamic sense of the process of resource capture, transformation and disposal) doubles approximately every 25 to 30 years. Early in the next century, the scale of activity will strain biospheric limits and even the capacity of the planet to sustain life.

Improved technologies can retard this process but cannot halt it altogether. Several signs indicate that the competitive market system is already causing certain natural thresholds to be crossed, including some which may not be recognised by political authorities until too late. Some of these thresholds are well known: the disappearing ozone layer, man-made climate change, collapsing fishing grounds and the like.

Among the palpable and immediate economic costs of human interference in natural systems is the increasing frequency of severe tropical storms, associated by many scientists with global warming. Hurricanes are the most expensive natural disasters in America and forecasters now believe their resulting cost could soar to new heights.

The world's major insurers have recognised the greatly increased frequency of these 'natural' disasters as a significant and potentially unsustainable financial drain on their industry. They now propose novel financial instruments in the hope of offloading future costs of claims to the investing public willing to wager that catastrophic storms will not occur.

Ecological tensions will also lead to greater political instability and more armed conflicts. Perhaps 70 per cent of the world's population already lives in 'water-stressed' areas. 'Eco-conflict' will occur first in the Middle East, Sahelian Africa and Asia, subsequently touching better endowed regions, with unpredictable results for the economy.

Giant corporations, wealthy communities and rich individuals, whatever their assets cannot escape the consequences of ecological degradation. Yet even they seem powerless to halt the process. They illustrate the paradox of beneficiaries unable to protect the system that benefits them, a paradox we shall encounter frequently in this Report.

At its heart lies the problem of the 'free-rider'. Whereas only some would pay the costs for turning these destructive trends around, all would benefit. If one company stopped trawling in order to allow fish stocks to recover, some less scrupulous rival would move in, take whatever fish remained and ruin the more ecologically responsible firm in the bargain. Short-term interests are paramount.

No one wants to go first, so all end up going last. Entrepreneurs do not want powerful states which can impose stringent rules on business, much less a global government, so no one regulates. No one can afford to stop and turn around, so destruction continues. Yet no one can live on a dead planet.

Pernicious Growth

To say that the free-market economy is threatened by growth sounds mad or heretical. 'Everyone' knows that growth is the motor of our economies and that no growth implies stagnation and decline. To risk a metaphor, just as the traveller in the harsh environment of the Sahara or the Arctic must keep moving forward or risk annihilation, so the voyagers on the market's great journey cannot stand still.

To stop is, sooner or later, to be shouldered aside and eliminated, to die by the wayside. Growth has thus become the system's never-ending quest, yet much of what passes for growth now reflects counter-productive, even harmful and destructive trends. The concept must be re-examined and redefined. The distinction between 'growth' and 'welfare' must be sharpened. Bigger and more do not necessarily mean better.

Let us take a trivial example from the American press: according to US insurance industry figures, automobile theft in 1995 cost $8 billion; that same year motorists installed $675 million worth of electronic devices in their vehicles in order to thwart thieves. This market is expected to reach $1.3 billion by 2000. It is rather short-sighted to exclaim, 'But this is good, since the auto-equipment industry will expand!'

Such economic activity is nonetheless registered as 'growth' in the Gross National Product (GNP), as are treatments for cancer, prison construction, drug rehabilitation centres, repairs occasioned by terrorist attacks and so on. The most efficient way to increase GNP rapidly is probably to wage war.

Although growth once correlated closely with increases in overall welfare, this is no longer the case. More and more economic growth is occasioned by social phenomena that most people would rather do without. Precise measurement of growth based on corrections or repairs of past failures is impossible but we stress the urgent need to examine this economic paradox in a new and harsher light.

Instead of welcoming growth for growth's sake, we should calculate its total costs, including the ecological and social ones, now externalised by those to whom the financial benefits of pernicious growth accrue.

Social Extremes and Extremism

The future of the free market also depends on who receives the benefits of growth. If the rewards are aimed at the bottom half of the population, these relatively poor people will use their money overwhelmingly for consumption and will keep demand buoyant. If the rewards go to the top of the social scale instead, the recipients will place ever greater sums in financial markets rather than in goods and services. As a result, demand will fall, bringing with it the dangers of rising inventories, over-production and stagnation. The nature of income distribution is therefore crucial to the longer-term well-being of the system.

Therein lies the danger: deregulated, competitive economies, while benefiting many, benefit those at the top most. Evidence from a broad variety of countries is overwhelming on this point: following liberalisation and deregulation, the top 20 per cent improve their position. The closer they are to the summit, the more they gain. The same law applies in reverse to the remaining 80 per cent: all lose something; those worst off to begin with lose, proportionally, the most.

Sharp social divisions and 'class struggle', as Marxists perhaps still call it, constitute a genuine menace. Beyond a certain threshold, disparities are dangerous for the system and must be carefully monitored. The fact that great differences in wealth and living conditions can provoke rage, disruptive behaviour and violence is hardly news but the late twentieth century has added a new wrinkle to this age-old truth: the tendency of the information-rich to provoke the rage and violence of the information-poor. The information-poor are a globe-spanning category and may or may not be the same as the materially poor.

The information-poor, precisely because they cannot produce, absorb or manipulate information in sufficient quantities or with sufficient speed have become dysfunctional when they have not been socially discarded. Their willingness to work, their muscle-power, is increasingly irrelevant in the computerised age.

Some rich societies like the United States, in spite of sharp wealth divisions between social strata, still seem able to absorb class frictions, though the existence of thousands of self-contained, walled and gated private communities reveals a profound apprehension. It is not clear how much longer this relative tranquillity may continue, particularly when the middle classes can no longer count on social benefits once supplied without direct financial outlay, such as satisfactory public schools and safe neighbourhoods.

In the European Union, although social extremes are less glaring, chronic unemployment, stagnation of wages in the lower brackets and the prevalence of temporary jobs (Continental Europe) or sharp increases in the number of 'working poor' (Great Britain) cause resentment and fear.

European governments are made and unmade on the issue of employment and their citizens are trying in vain to square the circle. Europeans want jobs but do not want to give up their social benefits in favour of more flexible labour markets. Many commentators have remarked on the 'vanishing middle' and the anxiety of middle-class people who live in dread of losing their own security and that of their children. 'Globalisation' is increasingly blamed for this state of affairs.

In many Third World countries, particularly in Latin America where extremes of wealth and poverty have always been the norm, the benefits of affluence are already offset by its drawbacks. Private security guards are indispensable, children of rich parents cannot go to school unaccompanied for fear of kidnapping, businesses must pay protection money, women cannot wear jewellery on the street, jogging or bicycling is impossible, driving one's own car or taking a taxi is risky but public transportation unthinkable, and so on.

The rage of the poor everywhere is augmented by televised fantasies featuring opulent lifestyles (usually accompanied by flagrant 'immorality' of behaviour). Millions take these soap operas seriously; they further believe that wealth is finite, unjustly appropriated by the dissolute few and therefore 'stolen' from the deserving many, including themselves.

Other disparities may be completely irrelevant to the rage–violence dialectic. One example frequently cited by moralists concerns the 450-some dollar billionaires who are said to be 'worth' as much as perhaps two and a half billion people in the Third World (as measured by their average per capita share in the GNP of those countries).

The billionaires versus the billions comparison is irrelevant to the continuing success of the free market because world wealth is not finite but elastic and, so far at least, constantly growing. The fortune of the billionaire is not perceived as stripped from the poor because the two groups do not inhabit the same physical space. The two and a half billion are most unlikely to meet the 450 billionaires or to stake a claim to their assets, but, even if they tried, they could not enforce that claim.

Physical contiguity of winners and losers makes the lives of the former far less pleasant than they ought, by rights, to be. But for paradoxical reasons, even in cases of severe hazard, winners rarely advocate redistribution of wealth to losers, although by doing so they might significantly lessen the risks to themselves. The winners' motto remains, as it has ever been, *Après nous, le déluge*.

Meanwhile, Western politicians invoke 'family values' in the mistaken belief that these values may somehow serve to hold together societies undergoing increasing stress. They do not explain how masses of people can adapt instantly to unemployment, inferior or precarious working conditions, geographical dislocation and longer hours while simultaneously devoting the requisite time and attention to their families. In most North American or European families, both parents now work in order to make ends meet. Thus the contribution of the family to social stability is also weakening.

In a climate of privatisation and the downgrading of state services, people are expected to take more responsibility for their local communities and their own poorer compatriots. Again, it is not clear how people who must necessarily compete and put their self-interest first and foremost throughout their working lives can radically change their mentality and devote themselves to the disadvantaged and the downtrodden in their 'spare' time.

Inexorable economic pressures combined with fraying social fabrics indicate that we are not merely entering another era of 'haves' and 'have-nots' as in the Great Depression. Our world is that of the Ins and the Outs. Optimists insist that there will be far more winners than losers, more Ins than Outs. We see social integration – bringing vast numbers of Outs in – as a formidable challenge to the system's resilience.

Just as citizens of the same country are distributed along the continuum of wealth<->poverty and security<->insecurity, so entire geographical regions are subject to the disparities generated by liberalisation and global competition. These regions also qualify as 'winners' or 'losers'.

South-eastern England and some neighbourhoods of London are booming whereas much of the North is wasteland and other areas of the capital are in decay. The United States' 'rust belt' stands in sharp contrast to more dynamic areas of the South and West. At the global scale, 'Tiger' or 'Dragon' Asia was typically regarded as a 'winner' area. As we complete our Report, however, the deepening financial crisis may relegate these countries to a lower rank. Africa qualifies as the quintessential loser.

Whether 'losers' react psychologically by blaming themselves and their leaders or by blaming others and refusing to accept guilt and responsibility for their loser-hood, sooner or later they attempt to compensate for their deficiencies. The means they choose may range from individual suicide to mass immigration; from political protest and peaceful demonstrations to the formation of private militias and outright terrorism.

Whatever the individual or collective strategies, losers are invariably destabilising for the prevailing or dominant system. Organised or diffuse protest against inequalities must be taken seriously and planned for, economically, culturally and, where appropriate, militarily.

The twenty-first century will have to tread an extremely fine line between preserving the necessary market freedom and preventing or containing the social side-effects that this freedom cannot help but engender. Otherwise, costs will soon outweigh benefits even for those at the top of the scale geographically and financially.

Gangster Capitalism

Large-scale crime can sap the foundations of legitimate economic activity. In particular since the dissolution of the Soviet Empire and China's adoption of some aspects of the market economy, 'gangster capitalism' (as one business magazine has called it) has taken over large areas of the globe and threatens many others. Parallel economies based on drug trafficking, arms smuggling, money laundering and corruption of all stripes are now valued in the trillions of dollars and attract new recruits hourly.

Huge areas of the world already lie outside the jurisdiction of any state. Legitimate authorities do not necessarily know, much less control, the location of private airports, cocaine-producing factories or cartel headquarters. These cartels have acquired not merely financial but also strategic power: it is widely rumoured that one powerful Latin American drug baron blackmailed a legitimate government by threatening to shoot down its commercial airliners from his private base using missiles that he had purchased on the clandestine arms market.

As gangs and mafias extend their reach, money and politics follow them. Legitimate businesses are sucked into their vortex. Gangs can afford to buy the requisite elements of national governments as convenient.

High-ranking Mexican officials of the 'war on drugs' turn out to be in the pay of the drug barons who also employ former US Green Berets, pitting their counter-insurrectional experience against the police and the FBI. Army officers in former Soviet Union Republics enhance their pitiful salaries through stolen arms (and probably nuclear) deals. Displaced tin miners in Bolivia are only too happy to work as cocaine growers and processors. Vast unemployment feeds this trend: covert organisations can recruit whatever manpower they need, including private armies.

Heavily indebted countries earn far more by exporting drugs, small arms or immigrants than by exporting legitimate primary commodities. Some analysts regarded the Russian–Chechen war as a conflict between rival gangs for control of strategic resources. Large outlaw economies like Russia's could tilt in any direction; unpredictable alliances between former Soviet Union Republics or ethnic groups and radical Islamic States could conceivably corner a significant portion of the world's oil supply.

Deregulation, desirable in itself, could come full circle and defeat its own initial purpose. Lucrative, parallel 'gangster capitalism' could become truly explosive, a clear and present danger to the legal market system. If it succeeds in supplanting legitimate business, traditional rules of competition would be blasted to bits, while corporate terrorism would become the order of the day. Today's relatively predictable business climate would be replaced by durable anarchy and a Hobbesian war of all against all among individuals, firms and nations.

Financial Meltdown

The risks of a major financial accident are intensifying; we are in fact surprised that it has not yet occurred.[4] Here we shall flag the inherent volatility of financial markets as a grave threat to the market economy.

World stock market indexes like the Dow-Jones, the FTSE, the CAC-40 or the Nikkei are narrowly based. In terms of the weight of their respective capitalisations these indexes rest on the fortunes of an extremely limited number of giant transnational corporations, perhaps 50 or 60 in all. Derivatives markets are now valued in the tens of trillions of dollars, at least in notional terms, well beyond the GNP of the United States, the largest national economy in the world.

Although the market may be at most times, in most places, inherently wise, it has, historically, displayed periodic attacks of insanity and mental breakdown endangering the entire system that our Report has been commissioned to defend. This danger is greater than at any time in the past, and thus an issue of paramount concern to be tackled in greater detail in the following chapter.

Underscoring the Contradictions

Simply stated, the Commissioning Parties have asked us if the global economic system is safe from major harm, if it is moving in the right direction to avert danger and, if not, how it might be protected. The threats to this system as outlined above all contain paradoxical aspects. Their inherent contradictions do not bode well for its continuing safety:

- The market is the best judge of the wisdom and value of human economic activity, but the market cannot tell us when we may be crossing ecological thresholds until it is too late.

- Growth is the economy's lifeblood but general well-being no longer necessarily correlates with growth, which in many cases is increasingly counter-productive, impoverishing rather than enriching.

- The economy is at the heart of society, but undesirable social effects may prove strong enough to undermine economic benefits. Business must remain free to invest and to prosper wherever conditions are most suitable, but people left behind will behave in unpredictable and destabilising ways. Over-regulation must be avoided but a wholly unregulated (or 'self-regulated') market risks self-destruction because, left to itself, it will create too few winners and too many losers, more Outs than Ins.

- Parallel, 'outlaw' economies are gaining strength both financially and politically; alliances between gangs and rogue states could create geo-political upheavals which would destroy the normal business climate.

- In the late nineteenth century, Walter Bagehot said, 'People are most credulous when they are most happy.' In the late twentieth century, John Kenneth Galbraith said, 'Financial genius is always before the fall.' Financial markets are inherently unstable and cannot be counted on to behave with perfect rationality: they too can create losers on a scale which would today make the 1930s look like a bad day at the races.

The dangers facing the market system require urgent attention. We shall now address the modes of control and protection established so far.

1.2

Control

The global economic system is threatened on all sides. Taken separately, the dangers may seem distant, but this is to disregard the ever-present threat of *positive feedback conditions*. Should several of these threats be brought to bear on the system at once, concentrating their impact like a laser beam on particularly sensitive nodal points, the system as a whole could reach a *critical state* and experience a *landslide effect*, culminating, perhaps, in a *global accident*.

These concepts must be grasped as directly applicable to safeguarding the global free market in the coming century; Let us supply one analogy: in nature, many single, local species extinctions can precipitate without warning a mass extinction. In the market system, specific, isolated failures could lead sequentially and synergistically to a cataclysm.

Eminent scientists explain that 'large interactive systems perpetually organise themselves to a critical state in which a minor event starts a chain reaction that can lead to a catastrophe'. 'Self-organised criticality' applies to both the natural and the economic spheres because the global market is a prototypical 'large interactive system'. The timing of such a 'minor' but critical, precipitating event is unpredictable; we have nonetheless entered the realm of the 'sooner or later'.[1]

We may place the 'critical state' in the even broader context of what philosopher Paul Virilio has called the 'global accident'. As he explains, the most brilliant, advantageous, useful invention in the world, whatever its nature, embodies its own specific, inherent, virtual accident.

Thus the invention of the airplane implies the simultaneous invention of the crash; nuclear power means meltdown; the computer carries with it the possibilities of catastrophic information loss and fraud; stock markets and other fora of exchange or speculation eventually lead to bursting financial bubbles, and so on.

Capitalism, to use its scientific name, is not the natural state of mankind. Rather, it is a product of cumulative human ingenuity, a social construct and, as such, perhaps *the most brilliant collective invention in all history.*

For the first time, the world (and our Working Party) is confronted with a crucial question: does the very success of this global invention imply that somewhere in the future lurks the global accident, the one from which the system and the world economy might not recover?

We cannot answer this question, but it points us to others to which it is our mandate to reply:

- Is the global system now protected?

- Are our present institutions sufficient to the task?

We reply in the negative. The means so far devised for overseeing, safeguarding and perpetuating the free market and the globalised economy are grossly inadequate.

Inadequate Institutions

A brief inventory of existing global institutions shows that most of them are worthless for escaping the dangers on the horizon. They may be worse than useless in so far as they convey a false sense of security. We live today in a tragically under-managed world.

The Predecessors

A few post-First World War international organisations have survived to this day, for instance, the International Labour Organisation (ILO), but they act, at best, as coordinators rather than as regulators. A handful help to regulate strictly circumscribed, technical areas of scant economic significance (for instance, the International Postal Union).

The Bank for International Settlements (BIS)

Founded in Basle in 1930, the BIS is often called the Central Bankers' Central Bank. It acts as an international clearing house, provides a forum for international monetary cooperation, centralises data and issues guidelines. This lessens the fears and the likelihood of a ripple effect after major banking failures (Bankhaus Herstatt 1974, Drexel Burnham 1990, BCCI 1991, Barings 1995).

The BIS is perhaps the best candidate for regulating financial markets but it does not do so today. In fact, it lacks all coercive power and market operators invent new financial instruments faster than this bank can deal with them.

The sheer mass of transactions might normally be expected to cause apprehension, yet according to the BIS, the 'official view remains that existing regulations, complemented by further efforts to improve internal controls, external transparency and market functioning, should be sufficient to contain systemic risks'.[2] We are far less sanguine.

The Bretton Woods Institutions

Founded in 1944 at the famous Bretton Woods (New Hampshire) Conference, these 'twins' are the World Bank and the International Monetary Fund (IMF). They have proved invaluable in instituting and enforcing economic discipline in the southern hemisphere and, to a lesser extent, in the republics of the former Soviet Union and its satellites. At the end of 1997, they began to perform the same functions in hitherto financially sovereign South-East Asian countries like Thailand, Korea and Indonesia.

Heavily indebted countries have had little choice but to apply structural adjustment programmes devised by the Bank and the Fund. Like it or not, dozens of these countries have liberalised their economies, privatised their state-owned companies, abolished exchange controls, increased their participation in world markets and, in most cases, continued to service their debts.

These are notable achievements and the Bretton Woods organisations should be credited with these accomplishments: they have been instrumental in hastening and deepening the process of economic globalisation.

The world has nonetheless changed drastically since these twins were born at the end of the Second World War. The Bank and the IMF are also suffering from 'mid-life crisis'. Set up to distribute funds, either for financing development projects or for smoothing out temporary balance of payments problems, they face increasing competition from financial markets and private investors.

For the most part, corporations and banks decide where their investments will best prosper and which Southern or Eastern governments deserve loans. The Bank and the Fund are in this sense victims of their own success: they have energetically promoted liberalisation and the market economy in their client countries, to the point, perhaps, of working themselves out of a job.

The Bank is doubtless more vulnerable in this respect than the Fund. Still, everyone wants them back in the picture when markets go wrong and they remain vital for channelling public funds to private investors when the latter massively miscalculate. Whenever the 'too big to fail' rule applies, the Bank and the Fund come into play as they have done in the crises of Mexico, Russia and Asia. Few people understand that their taxes serve to bail out not the governments in question so much as the big private players on these markets.

The twins must now concentrate on adapting more rapidly to new conditions. Like the rest of the 'foreign aid industry', the International Development Association (the 'soft-loan' arm of the Bank funded by grants from national governments) should expect to receive ever-dwindling contributions from its erstwhile donors. The Bank has already grasped that it must become more closely allied with market forces and is consequently upgrading its private sector cooperation wing (International Finance Corporation; Multilateral Investment Guarantee Agency). With regard to its more traditional lending, the Bank will need to emphasise advice to private enterprise and act as broker between governments and business.

The IMF can be relied on to take its traditional hard line with regard to debt relief and fiscal orthodoxy and to maintain the discipline of structural adjustment in countries beholden to it. On the other hand, it would be foolhardy to count on the Fund or the Bank to stem or even to predict a financial accident of calamitous proportions.

These institutions, the employers of several thousand highly trained, generously paid economists, deeply involved for decades in Mexico, failed to foresee the Mexican financial crisis of December 1994, or, if they foresaw it, failed to warn of its imminence. Similarly they failed to anticipate the dramatic and market-jolting turmoil in Asian financial markets in 1997.

At the behest of the United States, the IMF contributed heavily to salvaging Mexico once the financial debacle was unleashed; it has broken all its own rules to keep Russia afloat with new loans and as we conclude our Report, it has begun to provide massive loans to the Asian 'tigers'. Its resources are, however, neither unlimited nor elastic.

We fear that the international economic community, should it rely too strongly on the IMF for predicting, much less containing, systemic risk, would be leaning on a hollow reed. Either the Fund must be voted much larger sums with which to stem potential disasters or it must be supplanted by a more competent institution. The Fund should, in particular, be less self-satisfied and stop relying on dogmatic ideology in the place of solid research so that it becomes institutionally capable of sounding the alarm when required.

We neither foresee nor recommend the immediate closure of the Bretton Woods Institutions. They continue to serve as the guarantors of liberalisation, privatisation and structural adjustment in large parts of the world; a task which no individual Northern government or group of governments should consider undertaking directly. They also remain useful, particularly to the G-7 countries, because they preclude the need for the latter to intervene overtly in the affairs of other 'sovereign nations' undergoing financial crisis.

The United Nations (UN)

A discussion of global safeguards and management must refer, at least in passing, to the United Nations. Although it has in a few instances creditably discharged its peacekeeping functions, we see no hope in other areas for genuine regulatory powers ever being conferred by major member states on the General Assembly or on the UN specialised agencies.

Of these agencies, UNICEF has perhaps been most successful since most governments can agree that vaccinating children is a worthy endeavour. Other UN bodies, working in more controversial or sensitive areas, have virtually no authority and will not be given more in future. For example, the Food and Agriculture Organisation (FAO) exerts no control over world production and distribution of food supplies; the UN Environment Programme (UNEP) is wholly ineffectual in preserving the environment, the UN Commission on Trade and Development (UNCTAD) makes no trade rules, and so on.

The UN is useful mainly because it is the one international forum which gives the smaller, weaker members of the 'international community' the illusion that they have something to say about running global affairs.

An innovation with possibly far-reaching consequences is the Ted Turner billion dollar mega-grant to the UN. Turner's personal generosity and altruism aside, the gift marks a philanthropic first in the privatisation of international, intergovernmental agencies and could set a precedent for further individual or corporate charity which could collectively shape UN policy. While this is a positive step, we regret that it may simultaneously appear to exonerate the United States from paying its long overdue contributions to the UN. For reasons to be made clear in due course, this is not the time to neglect one's international institutional responsibilities.

The World Trade Organisation (WTO)

The WTO is a more promising candidate for international success. This relative newcomer, which replaced the General Agreement on Tariffs and Trade – GATT – on 1 January 1995, is perhaps a harbinger of a new world order, since its member governments have endowed it with authentic decision-making and regulatory powers. The WTO is welcome news for those who hope to sustain free-market globalisation and we applaud it as a major step forward.

Under WTO rules, individual member countries can no longer impede trade. Should they try to do so, they become subject to permanent sanctions. As the *Wall Street Journal* put it with admirable directness, the WTO 'represents another stake in the heart of the idea that governments can direct economies'. The director of this organisation scarcely exaggerated when he proclaimed, 'We are writing the constitution of a single global economy.'

Under WTO laws, trade-restrictive practices are banned and non-tariff barriers, even if they are labelled as measures to protect human health or the environment, may be challenged by any WTO member nation. WTO panels, not national courts, hear disputes and make binding decisions.

This is the first time that an international institution has been empowered to supersede and strike down particular national interests, even when these are enshrined in law or custom. 'Each Member shall ensure the conformity of its laws, regulations and administrative procedures with its obligations [to the WTO]', says its charter agreement. This obligation concerns past, present and future laws.

Such an international regulatory body risks provoking serious contradictions. The richer, more democratic and the poorer, more autocratic countries already disagree fundamentally on issues of labour rights or environmental protection and their relationships to trade.

Backlash in the rich countries may also occur. Citizen-consumers may react with outrage when they discover that WTO rules oblige their nations to accept much lower standards than those to which they had been accustomed. Areas as crucial to them as food, health, safety and the environment are certain to be affected; developed nations will be required to admit the goods of the less developed ones even when these were produced under dubious sanitary or ecological conditions.

A few random examples illustrate the point: markets will offer consumers fruits, vegetables or wines containing pesticide residues (some considered carcinogenic) far higher than those now allowed by most European or North American national laws. Europeans may be obliged to accept meat from US beef cattle raised on bovine growth hormone or genetically modified feedstuffs. Bans on trade in asbestos, toxic wastes or driftnet fishing could be rescinded, food labelling requirements waived and many products containing unsafe substances legalised.

Consumer and environmentalist organisations may become more vocal as these realities sink in. Citizens are also likely to resent the WTO's dispute resolution procedures since its panels meet without observers and their documents, transcripts and proceedings are not disclosed.

Under the old GATT rules, trade sanctions could not be imposed upon any member country without the unanimous approval of all the others. This procedure was far too weak and virtually guaranteed that no member need fear sanctions. The WTO takes matters in the opposite direction. Sanctions apply automatically to the party found guilty by its panels unless member countries vote unanimously against them within 90 days.

To sum up, despite an uncommon success or two like the WTO and a few advances towards binding policies in the global arena, the international regulatory sphere is full of gaping holes. If it is to be self-sustaining, *a globalised economy needs rules*. Those rules can best be made by the major actors in that economy.

The Role of Transnational Corporations

These giant companies could and should provide many of the necessary political control mechanisms to insure the permanence of the system that guarantees their existence and their profits. This they have scarcely recognised, although they have begun the task of consensus-building with international leaders in venues like the annual Davos meeting of the World Economic Forum or the Transatlantic Business Dialogue.

These companies may decide in future that competition is all very well but not conducive to the proper conduct of their affairs. The oil industry best fits this pattern: it has largely renounced competitive behaviour in favour of *de facto* collective management of production, distribution and prices. Other industries may well come to terms with each other internationally as they did nationally during the late nineteenth and twentieth centuries, so as to avoid cut-throat competitive tactics detrimental to all.

We fear, however, that this day is still far off. Despite some spectacular recent mergers, European, American, Japanese and other transnational players continue to compete fiercely for world market shares. In so doing, they further destabilise an already fragile global system. Industries as diverse as automobiles, chemicals or pharmaceuticals have suffered from the creation of huge over-capacity in recent years. Each giant corporation attempts to gain a temporary advantage through investments in cutting-edge technologies with the minimum input of labour.

Too many remarkably efficient factories are consequently producing *too many* goods for *too few* solvent purchasers. At the same time that companies are sacking their workers, they are 'downsizing' their customers as well. No replacement for Henry Ford's wisdom has yet been found: pay your workers enough so that they can purchase your cars.[3]

Since it is mathematically impossible to sell all the automobiles (and many other goods) now produced, major shake-outs are bound to occur, yet companies continue to close down modern factories in order to build even more modern ones elsewhere, generally employing fewer and cheaper workers in the process.

These same patterns obtain in nearly all manufacturing industries and gluts will be exacerbated by recent Asian setbacks as companies sacrifice everything to exports in order to pay off their debts. Meanwhile, Asian customers will be buying far less. So far, the response of transnationals to industry-wide oversupply has consisted not in cooperation but in further competitive moves. They are engaged in a continuing and ultimately doomed effort to gain temporary advantage over each other. Chronic over-capacity was one factor which led to the Great Depression of the 1930s; most of the elements are now in place for another.

The environment supplies further proof of the refusal of these companies to take their regulatory responsibility seriously. In 1992, the United Nations hosted the UN Conference on Environment and Development (UNCED) in Rio de Janeiro. Prior to the Rio Conference, the World Business Council for Sustainable Development, founded by several dozen transnational corporations (TNCs), worked closely with the conference secretariat in order to preclude any discussion of a binding or non-binding environmental Code of Conduct for TNCs. They argued that they could and would take responsibility for their own environmental stewardship.

The conference thus left environmental regulation and management entirely to individual governments, whereas the companies are by definition transnational and most environmental problems are trans-boundary. The Rio Conference, the only high-profile international gathering to have issued any environmental guidelines at all (the so-called Agenda 21) thus tacitly recognised that transnational corporations should be individually self-regulating.

Some experts and company spokespersons say that they can, as a group, contribute to preserving the environment. In spite of a few encouraging examples, we see little evidence supporting this view.

Regulating Financial Markets

Existing international institutions and transnational corporations are for the most part unable, unwilling or incompetent to manage the market-based system as a whole. Given the threat of volatile financial markets and the predominance of finance capital on the international scene, we are led to ask if major financial actors might be persuaded to take on this role. Realistically, we see several factors militating against globally responsible behaviour on the part of the international financial industry.

Some observers have claimed that information technology is now powerful enough to foresee and forestall major accidents. We disagree: too many layers of complexity now exist. For the first time markets operate in a truly borderless world but the technologies that made this world possible have spread much faster than the means of protecting it from its own successes and excesses. The abolition and unification of time and space undermine stability.

Information technology places all operators in instantaneous and constant contact but cannot shield them from their own actions and can even contribute to provoking critical events. The role of 'programme trading' in the 1987 US stock market plunge provides an early if graphic illustration.

State authorities, even in the most powerful countries, no longer exercise full control over the value of their currencies and monetary policies. Foreigners hold massive stakes in government bonds (national debts) and can withdraw these investments at the slightest unwelcome signal, causing meltdown of financial reserves and jagged fluctuations in exchange rates. George Soros's billion-dollar *coup* against the British pound demonstrated that Central Banks are no longer a match for powerful speculators.

Not only are national financial markets fully integrated into the global one; the boundaries between different kinds of markets which used to be separate have also broken down. Recognisable frontiers can no longer be traced between short-term and long-term capital markets, foreign exchange markets, options, futures, commodities or derivatives markets, and so on. 'Leverage is all'; whole economies are literally based on paper representing purely notional values. Derivatives markets are expanding phenomenally. Invented to protect *against* financial risks, derivatives now heighten them.

Nor do financial markets maintain much connection with the 'real' economy or trade. Amounts circulating daily in foreign exchange markets routinely represent at least 50 times the entire market value of transactions in tangible goods and non-financial services.

A great conclave of major financial market operators armed with the latest information technologies could conceivably work to reduce the risks of accident but who is likely to take the initiative to call upon them? Who will be the artisans of financial disaster prevention? In most quarters, the mere possibility of global market accident is not recognised.

Individual speculators, corporations, banks, brokerage houses, pension funds, and so on, are reaping great benefits from the system yet they *do not and cannot care for the system itself*, whatever their own best longer-term interests. These operators are rational beings and the market is posited on the rational actions, knowledge and expectations of all participants. In the financial sphere, however, instantaneous decisions prevail; short-term logic works against long-term benefit, the immediate rights of each operator supersede the maintenance of the system which guarantees those rights. In such a context, how can one contain dangerous trends, much less prevent a serious, even global, accident?

Taxation of international financial transactions, even at barely perceptible levels, is scarcely discussed and is dismissed when it is. The sheer exuberance and volume of trading makes many people rich so it is not surprising that a basic law of human behaviour is at work: the law of maximum collective resistance to reining in that exuberance. A major financial accident would trigger massive business failures and hugely increased unemployment provoking social eruptions on a volcanic scale. A global financial crisis today would be far worse than that of 1929 – yet it seems impossible to plan for or to avoid.

Let us borrow another analogy from science. Some humans may be capable of altruism, of sacrificing themselves and their own immediate interests for the greater good of the whole. Biologists suggest that observed animal 'altruism' is based on maximising the chances of passing on one's own genes to future generations. The noted geneticist J.B.S. Haldane once wittily declared, 'I would lay down my life for three brothers or nine cousins.'

The bedrock of free-market theory and practice, need we remind the Commissioning Parties, is not altruism or self-sacrifice but immediate self-interest and profit. It would thus be astonishing to find this market rife with statistically significant unselfish behaviour. This holds true even when it can be shown that some policies and individual actions are much more likely to protect the system than others; to allow it to pass on, as it were, its genes. Market players care only about themselves, today, not about transmitting their individual or collective inheritance.

Looking at the matter in historical perspective, it is, or should be clear that the New Deal under President Franklin Delano Roosevelt saved American capitalism from almost certain demise and the United States itself from some form of radical populism, socialism or perhaps even national socialism. Had Roosevelt not intervened with a vigorous Keynesian programme, social breakdown, following on the heels of the 1929 stock market crash and already well advanced by 1933, could have demolished the liberal system in the world's most powerful economy today and its strongest defender of market freedom. Roosevelt ought to have been given a hero's welcome and a capitalist's blessing.

What one actually observed in the United States of the 1930s was deep distrust and even deeper hatred of FDR on the part of the American upper class. In many households, as one of us can personally attest, 'Roosevelt' was a dirty word, not to be pronounced in front of ladies, children or servants; one spoke instead of 'That Man'. The New Deal may have saved America, but it never pacified or convinced its most ardent opponents, whose antagonism has lasted to this day.

National authorities, if they tried to undertake Rooseveltian policies, would be immediately sanctioned by the markets. Global Keynesian policies, taxation of transactions and constitution of 'safety net funds' might forestall a serious accident and prevent widespread social upheaval, but those whose interests they would ultimately serve would not support them any more than the business and financial elites of the United States supported the New Deal. Consequently, no global redistributive or financial market regulatory policy is on the horizon and global authorities, such as they are, have little hope of reducing systemic threats.

One, Two, Many Global Markets ...

Although we have followed conventional usage and spoken repeatedly of 'the market', we are not actually in the presence of a single world market but of four overlapping and interlocking ones:

- The traditional market in *goods and services*

- The *labour* market

- The *financial* market

- The little-recognised *'environmental'* market (comprising land, tangible and intangible physical resources, plus the use of nature as a 'free' or paid receptacle for pollution and wastes).

A single transnational corporation routinely and simultaneously acts in all of these markets. It seeks the most productive labour at the most favourable cost; it constantly hedges to guarantee the value of its future transactions in a variety of currencies; it consumes natural capital and uses waste-dumping facilities; it sells goods and services. These activities cannot be put in airtight compartments even if they are carried separately on the company's books.

The 'market' deals in many 'goods' like human labour, body parts for transplant, genetic materials, water, land, air, hedge funds, warrants and options. None of these, in the strict sense, has been 'produced' by anyone.

As we hope to have shown, of these four interlocking markets *only the market for goods and services boasts even a semblance of orderly regulation at the global level* thanks to the World Trade Organisation. Regulation of the other three markets – for labour, finance and nature – is left mostly to chance and to the more or less rational forces of supply and demand.

It should come as no surprise that unregulated (or 'self-regulated') markets are quite capable of creating tensions (mass unemployment, social upheaval, environmental degradation, financial crash) that undermine the market system itself. Global shock-absorbers are not being installed on our standard model. Given an inherently fragile system lacking legitimate, enforceable rules, we can only warn against global accident some time in the early twenty-first century (if not before).

Such a conclusion, though it seems to the Working Party inevitable under present circumstances, is nonetheless unacceptable to us and we assume that it will also be unacceptable to the Commissioning Parties. For this reason we must face the paradoxes inherent in the system.

Liberty versus Limits

We believe that to be genuinely free, the market requires constraints. Today, the amount of care and protection expended upon the system's maintenance is inversely proportional to the degree of benefit derived from it. In other words, the worst threats stem from the largest players. Our only existing international regulatory institutions are all 'regulating' in the direction of *even greater freedom for the market to operate without constraints of any kind.*

A system based on individual freedom, self-regulation and 'Darwinian' competition and survival of the fittest will not suddenly turn around and, by and of itself, beg to be regulated. The system's chief beneficiaries cannot be expected or, under present circumstances, forced to act against their own immediate interests, against the very principles of profit and self-advantage upon which the free market and their own success are founded. To imagine that these beneficiaries might, in large or even significant numbers, recognise in time the need for external regulation is to deny all known laws of human behaviour. This contradiction must be underscored and faced.

All the threats to the global free market stem from its successes and from the most remarkable exploits of the Invisible Hand. The system's prime movers have demonstrated extraordinary resistance to discussing and confronting these threats honestly. In our view, were such escapist behaviour to continue, it could well prove fatal. Still, the near universal assumption of the principal market participants is 'the more freedom the better'.

Up to a point, yes. Just as we revere the works of a giant like Friedrich von Hayek, so we believe in the freedom of the marketplace. Despite this profound assent, we stress that without rules and constraints, the market can cause its own downfall. Left to itself, it will to create too few winners and too many losers; it will lead to over-production and under-consumption, to ecological destruction, to ever-increasing concentrations of wealth and ever-greater rejection of the unfit.

Whatever the prevailing rhetoric, the unregulated global marketplace will not work for the environment or for huge numbers of workers and potential workers, especially the billion-plus who are unemployed or seriously under-employed. The numbers of the unfit will inexorably rise until they make their presence felt in any number of deleterious and destabilising ways.

As the world becomes a single, unified market, adaptations which in the nineteenth century might have taken place over two or three generations must now be accomplished in a few short months or years. The pace of change has become overwhelming and Schumpeter's 'creative destruction' operates on the grandest of scales. Those who cannot or will not adapt quickly enough are instantly excluded from the system's benefits.

'Global Keynesianism' or 'Rooseveltianism' might be able to contain potential explosion and chaos but the 'Roosevelt Rule' states that players in a system based on short-term self-interest and the self-regulating market, believing fervently in the wisdom of that market, will reject regulation even when it can be shown to serve the system's, and their own, best longer-term interests.

The problem is not merely economic and psychological but political. Politics implies rules. Our present institutions cannot provide a political framework of universal dimensions. Our major market actors remain blind and deaf to their own, and the system's, interests. The Invisible Hand will strike back at those who have placed in it all their faith. We see only one way to escape this dilemma, to which we now turn.

1.3

Impact

So far we have voluntarily abstained from dealing with three major determinants of the future of the planet and the free-market system, namely consumption, technology and population. These factors can be combined in a single, simple equation:

Impact (on the earth) = Consumption x Technology x Population

$$I = C \times T \times P$$

This equation, frequently used by demographers, biologists and environmental economists,[1] is central to our demonstration. When the variables are correctly interpreted, it also renders social and economic predictions measurably easier since these three components, C, T and P, themselves incorporate many other variables such as wealth and poverty, level of economic development, health, education, fertility, status of women and the like.

If one accepts, as we argue one must, that the market economy is a sub-system operating within the total, or natural, system, then this equation points forcefully to the dangers ahead. A viable economic future within the constraints of the biosphere depends on:

- the number of people in the world

- the quantity, quality and nature of their consumption

- the technology employed to produce what they consume and to dispose of the wastes they engender.

Consumption

The 'C' variable, as one would expect, is particularly income-sensitive. The average Frenchman's consumption per capita is five and a half times that of an Egyptian; a German consumes

17 times as much as an Indian, an American 35 times more than a Tanzanian, and so on.[2]

Humanitarian organisations often express moral indignation over marked differences in consumption between North and South. This outrage is ill-directed. The average Swiss person may be able to consume 17 times as much as a Nigerian, but in a global market economy the only rational response to that fact is, bluntly stated, 'So what?' The Swiss are productive, their population is stable, they boast a high savings rate and their good fortune cannot be blamed on plunder or colonialism. On the other hand, if Nigerians do not choose to save, invest and improve their productivity, the only way for them to become richer and to consume more is for there to be fewer Nigerians. Nor is there an automatic conduit between the Swiss and the Nigerians. The former are in no way directly depriving the latter.

It is the vocation of humanitarians to disagree with these observations. They often urge Westerners to adopt the Gandhian principle of 'living more simply so that others may simply live' and they encourage cross-border sharing. Can one lessen the threats to the planet and diminish transnational social inequality by reducing personal consumption and transferring national wealth? The Swiss can always decide politically to deliver official aid to the Nigerians and individual Swiss people can base their economic behaviour on ethical choice. But how 'efficient' are such choices in economic or environmental terms?

Official development aid has proved powerless to diminish, much less close the North–South, rich–poor gap. On the contrary, disparities between them have widened since the Second World War when the wealth ratio was about 30 to 1. It is now 70 to 1 and rising. Since the end of the Cold War, aid has declined drastically and we confidently predict it will never return to previous levels. Even during its heyday, aid was mostly captured by the already affluent segments of the Third World population and affected the consumption of the poor marginally if at all.

Private charity fares no better. If a significant proportion of a rich country's population voluntarily renounced part of its material well-being in favour of sharing with Gandhian 'others' in the South, this attitude might be judged morally admirable but the people concerned would have no guarantees that the poor benefited from their altruism unless all the savings were sent to a worthy cause with an ironclad reputation for delivering.

Since the beginning of the 1990s, charitable contributions have outstripped official aid to Africa. Even so, total public and private aid is grossly inadequate to the task of allowing a great many others to live, simply or otherwise. Lower consumption in the North cannot be bottled or magically transformed into higher consumption in the South. Some well-meaning, ethically motivated people have become vegetarians in the belief that grain not converted into meat will somehow reach the world's hungry. They are mistaken: food is a commodity. If the monetary demand for grain or animals is reduced, less grain will be planted and fewer animals will be raised.

World-scale charity, probably since the first Christian missionaries, is a Northern specialty. In the southern hemisphere, one finds no recognisable religious or secular tradition of sharing with geographically distant or culturally separate peoples. Institutional charity is rarely practised and if it exists at all, begins at home.

Self-imposed restrictions, if channelled through charities, may ease individual distress but they will never equalise consumption between the well-off and the deprived nor will they alter total impact on the planet. Even if practised on a large scale, they could simply create a margin for greater consumption on the part of the less virtuous at home and abroad. This is because the consumption of elites in large parts of the South would be simultaneously rising and cancelling out the economic-environmental value of virtue in the North. Rising incomes automatically spell increased demand for all kinds of products, particularly in countries where masses of people have never before been able to vary their diet or to purchase a refrigerator, a television set or a motor vehicle.

Energy consumption reliably measures levels of economic development: the Asian 'dragons' all more than doubled their per capita energy use between 1980 and 1995. High-income countries consume three and a half times more energy per capita than middle-income countries and nearly 14 times more than low-income countries. Meat is the other item which invariably registers improved economic well-being. World consumption, particularly of meat (mostly grain-based) and energy (mostly fossil fuels) is destined to rise.

In any event, moral choice and charity towards the less fortunate, especially the geographically removed, has never determined mass behaviour and cannot, even under generous assumptions, be expected to balance incomes nor to counter an inexorable increase in the numbers of new, more affluent consumers.

Technology

Human impact on the environment varies with the physical nature of the assets consumed and the technology used to produce and dispose of them. Comparisons of energy consumption can be deceptive without introducing the technology 'T' factor. 'Poor-people's energy' like low-grade, sulphurous coal undoubtedly causes more direct pollution than nuclear energy. However, nuclear power may generate more CO_2 than coal when one takes into account the energy required for its entire cycle, including mining, enrichment, fission and waste disposal.[3]

At the other end of the consumption spectrum, people who use primitive tools to cut down 'free' trees for fuel may contribute less CO_2 to the atmosphere than Northerners burning oil or gas, but they simultaneously destroy huge swathes of forests that could otherwise absorb CO_2, preserve species diversity and prevent soil erosion. Wood still represents 50 to 90 per cent of all energy use in Africa.

Even improved technology cannot guarantee reduction of total planetary impact. Automobile engines are more efficient than they were 20 years ago but the number of cars on the road worldwide more than doubled between 1970 and 1990 to 560 million. More driving plus more traffic jams cancel out fuel efficiency gains. The same applies to other mass consumption goods: they may be less resource-intensive, lighter and more efficient but sheer numbers make such improvements self-defeating in terms of total impact.

Some observers believe that radical changes in present technologies will prevent irreversible damage to the planet. One can dream of roads teeming with hydrogen-powered cars, cities full of energy-efficient buildings, landscapes dotted with solar energy grids along with organic farms and zero-emission factories recycling each other's wastes. Such fantasies leave out politics and well-entrenched interests.

A multitude of alternative, inexpensive, low-environmental impact technologies already exist. Others could be easily developed. However, any attempt to promote rapid and massive switchovers from economies based on fossil fuels, chemicals, steel, and so on would provoke hostility and retaliation from the industries concerned, an entirely normal reaction. For them it is more profitable and convenient to stick with what they have already learned, developed and amortised than to strike out on new paths.

Politicians in both North America and Europe are highly attuned to such corporate interests. In the United States, at least $30 billion worth of subsidies are directed each year to energy industries alone. In Europe, powerful lobbies like the European Roundtable of Industrialists press for denser networks of road transport and shape EU policy towards deregulation. Whenever and wherever its present advantages and practices are under threat, industry naturally fights to maintain them.

Such actions will remain the norm even though safeguarding particular industrial interests is not conducive in the long run to preserving the system as a whole. Incentives to adopt radically cleaner, lower-impact and more efficient technologies are lacking too because consumers and taxpayers, rather than corporations, are now taxed to pay for dirty, inefficient ones. This will remain the case so long as industry can externalise these costs.

Today in the developing countries, most locally produced or imported technologies are rooted in the bygone years of the first Industrial Revolution. The poorer the country, the more reliant it is likely to be on outmoded 'sunset' industries and the dirtier and less efficient its technologies will be.

The World Trade Organisation, although valuable from a regulatory point of view, has virtually enshrined polluting and wasteful technologies in international law by refusing to allow discrimination between products on the basis of Processes and Production Methods ('PPMs' in the negotiator's jargon). This means that no country can refuse the goods of another, even if they were produced at the cost of significant ecological destruction.

Once more, because economic incentives to reduce waste and pollution are few, the rewards of trade are programmed to flow towards the dirtiest, least responsible producers in the South and to those most expert in externalising costs in the North. Even assuming that industry was prepared massively to accept conversion to lower-impact technologies worldwide and to embrace alternative solutions immediately, a North American or European middle-class standard of living would remain beyond the reach of hundreds of millions of people, if only because of the sheer physical limits of the planet.

Population

Our initial equation, Impact (on the planet) = Consumption x Technology x Population, can now be seen to hinge crucially on the 'P' factor.

The facts are well known but bear repeating:

- Twice as many people are now alive on earth as in 1970 when the population stood at less than 3 billion.

- Every year, some 175 million pregnancies result in approximately 133 million live births (the 42 million difference being chiefly due to legal or illegal abortions). World mortality is about 52 million a year, which means a present net population increase of some 81 million people annually (1995).[4]

- This means that (at least) 360,000 babies are born every day on average, more than 90 per cent of them in the Third World; adding to world numbers the equivalent of another Mexico every year, another India every 12 years. In contrast, 142,000 people die every day, many of them well beyond their reproductive years.

- Throughout history, mortality and fertility rates were virtually identical: as many people died as were born. Large numbers of human beings never reached reproductive age. Today fertility exceeds mortality by over 250 per cent. Infant and child mortality continues to fall and life expectancy to rise.

- More people will be added to world population in the 1990s than in any previous decade.

- Even if fertility declines markedly as it has already begun to do in several countries, population will continue to increase for decades to come because of the momentum based on age structures. At least one-third of all poor countries' present populations are under 15; in Kenya, fully 60 per cent of the population is under 15. The 'age pyramid' favours present and future childbearers.

- By the time the Commissioning Parties read this Report, world population will have reached 6 billion. It will attain 7 billion by 2008, 8 billion by 2020. Projections for following decades range from 9 to 13 billion, depending on the set of assumptions.

- The population of approximately 30 rich countries is stable or declining. In all the others it is still increasing, though usually at lower rates than a decade or two ago. Even the most optimistic global 'stabilisation' scenarios recognise that population will only level off at an extremely high level (10 to 12 billion) and that the levelling off will not in any case occur until 2050 to 2075.

Measuring Impact

A novel (if disputed) method for 'solving' the $I = C \times T \times P$ equation and predicting future planetary welfare is the method of the 'ecological footprint'. This method measures the quantity and quality of ecological resources needed to support a given population at a given level of consumption and technology.[5]

The footprint method divides productive terrestrial ecosystem surface area by world population. Even wilderness which should by rights remain untouched is included in the 'productive' category. According to this radically egalitarian calculation, in the mid-1990s every human being would be 'allotted' 1.5 hectares. Thus under conditions of absolute impartiality, each of the earth's inhabitants ought to make do with the productive capacity of 15,000 square metres (3.75 acres) or about one and a half football (soccer) fields.

The ecological footprint thus measures 'supply and demand' at its most basic. 'Supply' is given once and for all by the biosphere. It is tending to dwindle as deforestation, desertification, erosion, salinisation, and so on, continue to reduce the earth's productive land mass. 'Demand' varies with climate, season, personal or cultural preferences and above all according to wealth. Measured against this benchmark, the footprint of the average North American measures four to five hectares, three times his or her 'fair' share of productive terrestrial resources. To satisfy their current requirements for food, forest products and energy, the Dutch are said to require 15 times more land than is available inside Holland.

Methodologically speaking, the footprint is an improvement on traditional evaluations of local 'carrying capacity' because it calculates total flows of matter and energy needed to support a given population at a given level of consumption. It thus incorporates factors like trade and urbanisation and makes geography a truly globalised science. But it also demonstrates that *anyone* with a reasonably decent lifestyle is now taking more than his or her 'fair' share, even though he or she is paying a fair, market-determined price for that 'privilege'.

As the South becomes more affluent, its consumption, and therefore its own ecological footprint, will grow. More disposable cash will necessarily create greater demand for housing, roads, shopping centres, and so on, thereby diverting 'terrestrial ecosystems' from immediately productive uses like growing grain for humans or animal feed. Resource squeeze is inevitable, not in the sense that the Club of Rome postulated in the 1970s (absolute scarcity of certain vital commodities like petroleum) but in the sense of planetary productive and absorptive capacity.

Scarcity of any kind has without doubt always stimulated human ingenuity. We dispute, however, the mainstream economic conviction that ingenuity can perpetually be a substitute for tangible physical resources. We deny too that late twentieth-century humans have managed to uncouple themselves from nature. It is not because we mostly live in cities that we weigh more lightly on the earth; it is not because we trade and import a high proportion of our matter-energy flows that these inflows can continue to increase without limit.

Whatever the methods of appraisal employed, all impartial observation points to the same incontrovertible facts: world consumption is slated to increase and technologies are not going to change with unprecedented, revolutionary speed. The complex systems upon which we as a species – and all other species – depend can take significant stress for a considerable time, but only up to a point, and not for ever.

Population and the Free Market

Huge annual population increases are not merely disquieting for ecological reasons. Paradoxically, they call into question the very theoretical foundations of the liberal society that it is our mandate to defend. According to the doctrine of *laissez-faire* and the seminal works of Adam Smith, individual decisions in the marketplace will have benign outcomes for society as a whole; each person pursuing self-interest will unwittingly contribute to the general good or what Smith called the 'public interest'. This postulate is the bedrock of liberal theory.

Yet here is the paradox: poor people in poor societies who are most responsible for the population explosion are usually having children for sound individual economic reasons. Destitute people in the South do not breed excessively out of sheer ignorance, carelessness or lack of access to contraceptives, though all these play a part. Feminists stress exploitation and the fact that poor, uneducated women are often forced to have more children than they want. This may well be true, but both they and the men exploiting them are still frequently profiting from the children they produce.

From the point of view of most poor Third World parents, a child brings in more than it costs. In rural settings, it helps with chores from an early age. In urban environments, some 250 million child labourers under the age of 14 help their families to survive. In extreme cases, children are sold outright, into prostitution, slavery or as sources of transplantable organs. In the absence of social security systems, children are expected to provide for parents in their old age. Children are also like lottery tickets: one may succeed in life and change the status of the whole family. Where infant mortality rates remain high, people have more children than they want to accommodate the probability of loss.

In a celebrated article of 30 years ago, Professor Hardin asked if *laissez-faire* could be justified in the area of reproduction. He failed, however, to note that for poor people, childbearing is *positively linked* to greater economic well-being.[6]

In the West, we now look upon a child as a costly undertaking whose benefits may be emotional but are surely not economic. Such was not the case in nineteenth-century European or American agrarian society when birth rates exceeded those in most Third World countries today. Nor is it the common view among those who now bear the most children.

The philosophical contradictions of the free-market system appear here in a harsher light. One must ask *who* has a right to participate in this system by making individually rational economic decisions. Is this participation a universal right? With regard to reproduction, is it normal and permissible or abnormal and illegitimate that each individual seeks to maximise his or her own advantage, given that children are usually an advantage?

We know for sure that hundreds of millions of individually justifiable decisions to have children will lead to the presence of a higher population than the planet can ultimately support. We also know with mathematical certainty that excessive populations in individual countries will result in increased pressure on land and other resources, the reduction of output per capita and therefore a drop in the standard of living.

Such effects can be offset if increasing returns to scale are guaranteed by scientific and technical progress, capital accumulation, improved management, higher investments in education and training, free trade and the like. Given such factors, larger populations *can* be richer populations, but what we have witnessed is rather a slow, not to say imperceptible, improvement in real income per head, so that the gap in living standards between rich and poor countries is constantly growing wider both in relative and in absolute terms.

This much is common knowledge. Less recognised perhaps is that huge population growth leads to equally huge disparities in the distribution of wealth in the overpopulated country itself. Too many hands seeking too little work depress wages, while scarcity of land and capital pushes up rents and profits. The country gets the worst of all possible worlds: high unemployment or, alternatively, starvation wages if nearly all hands are employed; plus over-rewarded property owners and deep disparities between the two groups.

Contrary to Adam Smith and to liberal doctrine, rational decisions to increase one's own economic welfare by producing offspring do not result in a benign outcome for society as a whole; at least if one defines that outcome as an improved situation for the worst-off themselves as a group. Although it will improve the absolute and relative position of the local elite, reproductive freedom does not serve the 'public interest' if this term is taken to mean upholding the liberal system, reasonable egalitarianism and the preservation of the planet. The Invisible Hand is thwarted by the Invincible Womb.

Reproductive power is real power. Poor people behave just as classical economic theory predicts: they try to create individual wealth, or at least potential wealth, in the only way that lies open to them. Their behaviour actually validates the intellectual foundations of capitalism but is in the end self-defeating because their standard of living as a group will be relentlessly depressed and the control exercised over them by the elite will be enhanced. If we wanted them to stop creating individual economic assets in the form of children, the logical course would be to redistribute other economic assets to the over-breeding classes worldwide so that they could invest in alternative wealth creation.

Sharing assets such as purchasing power, education, jobs, infrastructure and the like could rapidly help to stabilise and reduce population growth. However, all the trends point in the opposite direction. Far from being reallocated, wealth and wealth-producing assets are being increasingly concentrated at the top. Partly because of its own reproductive prowess, the bottom now makes do with proportionally less than ever before. And it can therefore be counted on to keep on producing its own lottery tickets.

The Consequences of Reproductive Freedom

The Commissioning Parties have asked us to explore how the liberal capitalist system can be best perpetuated. We intend to answer that question and no other; we will therefore not speculate on alternative systems or on alternative definitions of the 'general good' and 'the public interest'.

Different options might well require radical North-to-South and rich-to-poor redistribution of productive assets plus drastic, coercive and immediate steps to curb greenhouse gases, pollution and waste. We have already explained why such measures appear utopian under conditions of unregulated globalisation and market freedom.

In the absence of enforced economic redistribution and ecological conservation, the issue of reproductive freedom is paramount. It must first be examined in the light of the well-known Malthusian arguments according to which population pressures will ultimately self-correct, through famines or other natural phenomena. This may well be so. But in the two centuries since Malthus published his *Essay on the Principle of Population* (1798), several key qualitative changes have taken place.

- Malthus was never concerned with *world* population, only that of particular nations. Although some trade in foodstuffs took place in the eighteenth century, on the whole each nation had to rely on its own subsistence production and each government was responsible for feeding its own people. The size of total population relative to biospheric capacity was not an issue at the time.

- Globalisation has changed the nature of the population 'checks' Malthus relied on. We now have reasonably efficient world 'death control' but not birth control; unlike our ancestors, we practise global charity ('humanitarian aid') and famine relief with regard to poor and populous nations.

- The time-scale has changed. Runaway surges in population starting from high levels mean that we no longer have the leisure to wait for Malthusian self-corrections to take hold. Eight hundred million or more new people every decade will burst the dikes.

According to Malthus, population pressure also has a positive side. Without it, man would never have cultivated the earth or become civilised.

[I]f we ... consider man as he really is, inert, sluggish and averse from labour, unless compelled by necessity ... we may pronounce with certainty that the world would not have been peopled but for the superiority of the power of population to the means of subsistence ... Had population and food increased in the same ratio, it is probable that man might never have emerged from the savage state.

The Working Party warns that in today's globalised world, 'the power of population' over the 'means of subsistence' will not result in intensification of agriculture or emergence into civilisation from a savage state but in various kinds of predatory behaviour directed against those who have managed to amass wealth. Millions will not remain 'inert and sluggish' although they may be as 'averse from labour' as ever. They, and their leaders, will resort to appropriation by whatever means may be at hand because they will be incited and compelled to do so. It is illusory to rely on (arithmetically) increasing food production – assuming it occurs – to compensate for (geometrically) swelling populations. Here the Malthusian argument has lost none of its persuasive power.

From the 1950s until 1984, food production outstripped population growth. Since 1984, the opposite has occurred. During the decade of the 1990s, food production has grown by 0.5 per cent annually while population continues to rise by 1.4 per cent annually worldwide. Population is increasing in the 'less developed' countries by 1.7 per cent annually and in the 'least developed' countries by 2.6 per cent, but most of world food production takes place in the developed countries where population growth is only 0.3 per cent annually.

In Part Two of this Report, we shall return to the theme of subsistence versus population. For the moment, let us simply note that Malthus is not dead, even though he has been asleep during most of the post-war period. Most world leaders have also been lulled into slumber. Food shortages will come once more to the fore. When that occurs, they will affect the most vulnerable who will, in turn, create political crises and social instability.

The Commissioning Parties have asked us to display intellectual freedom and frankness and to refrain from sentiment. No

Working Party member cares to belong to the caste of 'coopted thinkers, the active and conceptive ideologues whose livelihoods chiefly depend on maintaining the illusions that the (ruling) class holds about itself', in the words of an out-of-fashion nineteenth-century philosopher.[7] For this reason, we will now without flinching draw the conclusions of the arguments developed so far.

1.4

Conclusions

Since the dawn of Western civilisation, leaders have been rightly concerned with population control. Plato cites the maintenance of a stable population as one of the principle duties of the rulers of *The Republic*. He goes on to provide elaborate guidelines for the eugenics applicable to various classes in order to improve the race, preserve numerical stability and ensure political equilibrium. Plato's instructions ensure that the upper classes – the brightest and best – will be given more opportunities to procreate than the lower orders.

In the fifth century BC, mortality was generally equal to or greater than fertility; war, disease and other accidents could wreak havoc and the leaders needed cunning to maintain the state at its ideal size with the optimum mix of inhabitants. To that end, says Socrates, the rulers will 'be obliged to make liberal use of lies and deceit for the good of the governed'.[1]

Today's rulers seem to have lost sight completely of the fundamental duty to maintain population stability, and, rather than lying to their citizens for their own good, they seem more often to be lying to themselves. Whether from cowardice or from ignorance, they pretend that the market can, by itself, bring happiness, riches and well-being to all, even in the face of staggering growth in the numbers of people pursuing these rewards. Thus the leadership continually transmits to the governed a subtle, unspoken and unexamined message: the neo-liberal economic order can embrace all people everywhere, no matter how numerous they are today or may become tomorrow. If, perchance, the economic order somehow leaves great numbers of these people out, this is due to momentary imbalances or malfunctions which will soon be corrected by applying the proper policies. Exclusion of anyone from the market's benefits is thus claimed to be temporary and should in no way be attributed to the nature of the system itself.

We contest this message. So, surely, do the most lucid of our 'rulers' if they have bothered to reflect at all on the nature of the free market and of our chosen economic system. The doctrine of liberalism is akin to that of the Gospels: many are called and few are chosen – although the market quite possibly applies a more generous policy than God. We maintain, rather, that global neo-liberalism *cannot* embrace everyone, not even in the most prosperous nations. It certainly cannot incorporate 6 or 8 billion people worldwide.

In former times, prior to globalisation, economic processes were essentially national and depended on addition. Production and distribution meant adding value by adding together various elements, essentially raw materials, capital and labour. According to Henry Ford's law, people were 'paid enough that they could buy your cars'.

In the era of globalisation, precisely because economic processes are international, they depend on subtraction. One adds value (profit) by using fewer elements, particularly labour, than one's foreign competitors. Labour is advantageously replaced by capital and information. When, as in the United States, labour costs still represent 70 per cent of all corporate expenses, international success *requires* cutbacks, reduction and rejection.

The lower the rate of ostracism, so to speak, from the system, the higher the costs of production and the lower the rate of profit. Conversely, the greater the degree of rejection of costly human elements, the higher the rate of financial return. This truth is reflected daily by stock markets where one witnesses securities' values increasing the moment a company announces major workforce redundancies ('downsizing').

The system cannot function without an ongoing struggle between products, firms and individuals. The fewer people entitled to share in the wealth, the greater the rewards to be distributed among the winners. Each person must compete not merely against his neighbours but against strangers thousands of miles away whom he will never meet.

Since profit is the goal and the motor of the system, corporations must be free to pursue it. The corporation belongs to those who have invested in its stock, its shareholders. Whatever the moralists may say, it does not belong to its employees, to its suppliers or to the town, city or country in which it happens to be located. This is doubtless as it should be, but one cannot have one's cake and eat it. The workforce, suppliers, local community and country will have to accept sacrifices.

Although rich nations will remain comparatively rich, not all their citizens can or will benefit from new wealth creation. Many will be left behind. As for the populations of poorer, more vulnerable nations, they will suffer varying degrees of widespread hunger and 'narrowspread' jobs, creating an increasingly explosive mixture.

In both richer and poorer countries, economic ostracism and the dialectic of the Ins and the Outs will give rise to destructive behaviour, including crime, mass migrations and terrorism. Large parts of the world, as we can already perceive, will be reduced to a Hobbesian state of nature. In the war of all against all, the state and sometimes even the market will be unable to function.

Our present leaders admit none of this, perhaps because it would require politicians to think the unthinkable. They are consequently lying to the governed, but above all to themselves.

Legitimate Population Growth?

We have posed the following question: is it *legitimate* that each person be free to seek his or her maximum personal advantage through reproductive power, whatever the consequences for the general good?

The notions of legitimacy and illegitimacy invoke law, authority and standards. With rare exceptions, population and family size have not been subject to national legislation or decree. If we try to place this question in the broadest possible context of legitimation, that of international law and the Universal Declaration of Human Rights of the United Nations, we find they have little guidance to offer.

Article 16 of this Declaration deals with marriage and the family and proclaims equal rights for married men and women. It affirms that 'the family is the natural and fundamental group unit of society and is entitled to protection by society and the state'. It says nothing about the size of that family. Nor does Article 25, which promulgates a veritable charter for the Universal Welfare State:

> Everyone has the right to a standard of living adequate for the health and well-being of himself *and of his family*, including food, clothing, housing and medical care and necessary social services, and the right to security in the event of unemployment, sickness, disability, widowhood, old age or other lack of livelihood ... Motherhood and childhood are entitled to special care and assistance. All children, whether born in or out of wedlock, shall enjoy the same social protection. [Our emphasis.]

Once more, the individual's reproductive power is deemed irrelevant: the super-abundant 'rights' proclaimed apply to 'himself and ... his family'. If that person has eight children and cannot afford to provide them with 'food, clothing, housing and medical care', then the duty to supply all these, according to the Universal Declaration, falls to society at large.

When the signatories of this Declaration met in 1948, world population stood at less than 2.5 billion. Already utopian then, it is entirely out of the question now to satisfy such 'rights' for 6 billion people, many of them destitute. In the 50 years since it was signed, the Universal Declaration has become a hopelessly contradictory document, for in Article 28, it also affirms that 'Everyone is entitled to a social and international order in which the rights and freedoms set forth in this Declaration can be fully realised.' The signatories clearly did not contemplate having to choose between unlimited individual reproductive freedom and a 'social and international order' (as well as an ecological one) now on the brink of collapse.

Yet thoughtful and responsible people, including Socrates and Plato, have known for millennia that uncontrolled numbers place unacceptable stress on the social order. Aristotle, too, points out that 'of all known well-ordered' states, not one has an 'excessive population'. For the citizens, good government implies 'excellence of order maintained among them' and 'excess in numbers does not lend itself to order'. If the *polis* is over populated, even the best laws will be to no avail and only 'divine providence' can then save it by providing order.[2]

Divine providence is unlikely to provide order in our earthly cities. The greater the excess in mankind's numbers, the more good government – and the declared purposes of the United

Nations – will be defeated, including the goal of a social and international order guaranteeing the very rights the UN champions. Swelling populations and human rights as conceived by the signatories of the Universal Declaration are mutually incompatible.

The Universal Declaration, while appearing to approve or condone the population explosion, is not accompanied by a corresponding authority or global institution which might legitimately intervene to curb it. Speeches at UN conferences are cheap. Binding contracts are never proposed nor are incentives offered. International bureaucracies exercise no moderating influence on population growth and nothing is to be expected at the intergovernmental level.

Nationally, a few states still directly or indirectly encourage unlimited reproductive freedom. In many poor and populous countries, the state uses its coercive power to maintain women in servitude and prevents contraceptives or even information from crossing its borders. Particularly retrogressive states persist in the mistaken belief that huge populations will ultimately make them more powerful. This was for example the case in Romania under the communist dictatorship and still seems to hold true in some Arab countries.

For the most part, however, in the South the state is simply overwhelmed. It often has no population policy worthy of the name. Many governments have gutted their public health and family planning budgets in response to demands for structural adjustment, debt repayment and financial discipline. Ironically, they often got into to debt in the first place by trying to prevent the drop in living standards which uncontrolled population growth engenders. A few governments, such as Indonesia and Chile, have undertaken serious campaigns to limit population growth. China tries to do so but the authorities are routinely disobeyed in both town and countryside. Millions of families exceed theoretical reproductive limits and the 'one child policy' is mostly honoured in the breach.

A strong preference for male offspring in most of the South creates a further impetus to high birth rates. In some regions of Asia, ratios of 130 boys to 100 girls are not uncommon. Who the extra 30 boys will marry is a question apparently not posed. Both the will and the means to curb the population explosion are lacking in countries where most of it occurs. Thus each year witnesses the arrival of tens of millions of human beings whose future prospects are even bleaker than those now facing their parents.

In the North the state is also deeply affected by the population crisis although it may not yet be fully conscious of the fact. As for containing it, the North has proved just as impotent as the South. The United States, fearful of offending anti-abortion (so-called 'pro-life') forces at home, refuses to sponsor population control in its international aid programmes. Private American foundations may attempt to fill the void but are no substitute for a vigorous foreign policy.

Many Ministries of Home Affairs in the OECD countries have become little more than Ministries of Immigration, yet they still do not know how to cope with their immigrant populations. These immigrants, at least for the first generation or two, are far more prolific than their native-born neighbours. The countries they flock to do not provide family planning programmes specifically targeted to their needs, much less reduce the incentives to bearing children, such as curtailment or termination of financial allocations or fiscal benefits as family size increases.

Immigrant families are larger and consequently poorer. They are often victims of inadequate schools and sub-standard scholastic attainment, inferior housing and virtual confinement in ghettos, lower skills levels and higher rates of unemployment. All these lead to their disproportionate activity in illegal trafficking of all kinds, gangs, petty crime and occasionally terrorism, often related to political conflicts in their countries of origin.

Although, to their credit, the vast majority of immigrants do not participate in illegal activities, they are still generally willing to work in the black economy for low pay, and without social protection. Illegal employees imply illegal employers, sometimes in league with international human-smuggling rings, tolerated by governments which recognise that their own firms need cheap labour to stay competitive. Eyes are closed, corruption spreads, crime goes unpunished and, rightly or wrongly, immigrant workers are perceived as competing for jobs and driving down wages.

Extremist politics flourish on both sides. Because they feel rejected in their adopted land, foreigners may seek refuge in exacerbated cultural and religious practices making them even less acceptable to the native-born population and creating a vicious circle.

These foreign residents, which Northern states already find difficult to assimilate into their mainstream, represent a mere fraction of those who will seek to migrate in future, as recurrent and widespread political, economic and ecological breakdowns strike their own societies. Since their remittances help to shore up the precarious finances of their home countries, their governments will make only half-hearted efforts to retain them, whatever promises they may have made to their Northern counterparts. Or, alternatively, these governments will black-mail Northern countries in exchange for preventing their citizens from leaving. One way or another, swelling populations will constitute a valuable export commodity.

Taken together, huge increases in numbers in the South and the expanding presence of Southerners in the North imply, sooner or later, grave cultural confrontations and implosions. The 'clash of civilisations' scenario pitting 'the West against the rest' has justifiably attracted considerable attention. Its origi-nator, Professor Huntington, himself stresses the fateful gap between the West's efforts to promote a universal Western culture and its declining ability to do so. The demographic dynamics are all on the other side.[3]

Perhaps because he finds the point obvious, Professor Huntington stops short of saying that the globalised free-market system cannot prevail if the culture that undergirds it becomes enfeebled. His work barely touches upon economics. Yet the culture of capitalism is predominantly Western, like it or not. Although the trader and the merchant have been with us throughout recorded history, the capitalist is of a different breed, one far less prevalent and dominant worldwide than many recognise. This breed is not Chinese, Arabic, Hindu, or even Japanese but Western, as historians like Fernand Braudel and Joseph Needham spent a lifetime demonstrating. 'Markets' and capitalism are not identical: markets can and do exist without capitalism (although the opposite is not true).

Capitalist culture internalises the notion of risk, the profit motive and the need to accumulate; it is not merely the culture of the merchant and the trader but of the saver, the investor and the entrepreneur as well. Had we to choose a single word to characterise this culture, it would be 'competition'. Love of struggle and willingness to venture into the unknown are at its heart; 'creative destruction' is its highest art. Yet the countries where free-market economics has shaped the dominant, capitalist culture for centuries will soon contain a scant 10 per cent of humanity. This constitutes an ominous portent for the system's future.

The prospect of cultural implosion within Western nations has received less attention than the danger of clashes across civilisational fault-lines. Professor Huntington is concerned with extended, culturally traced frontiers. In contrast, he devotes virtually no attention to immigration issues or intra-national conflict. Yet quite aside from routine and primitive ('skinhead') attacks on foreigners in Europe and America, there is a perverse dynamic at work which points to latent conflict at a deeper level which will eventually affect millions.

When, as is frequently the case today, assimilation of outsiders, or, for that matter, of the native-born, into a given national culture no longer takes place through schools, churches, political parties, the armed forces, civic associations, the workplace and the whole range of social institutions, it can only be mediated, willy-nilly, through advertising, television and overarching consumerism. All these are products of the free market.

The very notion of assimilation into a culture thus becomes contradictory. Whereas it costs nothing to attend school or church and costs only voluntary time to participate in an association or a political party, substantial disposable income is needed to participate in the mercantile culture. Millions lack that income, although they are constantly aroused and provoked by images of consumption.

Many social thinkers have remarked that shopping malls and commercial centres are the true cathedrals of our time; that the number of would-be worshippers grows daily. But not all souls can join in this communion of consumers. Outcasts are not just foreigners but the local unemployed, the working poor in ill-paid, dead-end jobs, the marginalised young or old; in a word, the losers, the Outs.

Inability to partake of the culture results in constant frustration which can only be expressed, sooner or later, in inner- or outer-directed rage. When their numbers reach a critical threshold, the Outs will provoke a cultural implosion; those who cannot be integrated seek solace – and often revenge – in various exacerbated and pathological forms of localism, ethnicity, fundamentalism and vigilante groups whose hatred is directed at the mainstream political culture. Private armed militias in the United States are only one example.

Sometimes sheer, 'senseless' destruction takes over. In certain European suburbs, teenagers have been known to destroy everything, including their own apartment buildings, schools, the clinics where their families receive free health care and the sports facilities placed at their disposal.

These trends all run counter to the conditions required for sustaining the global liberal system in the coming century. Let us list succinctly the conditions for continuing success:

- Reliable and remunerative employment must be guaranteed to a far higher proportion of the population than is the case today. Although the task of the free market is not to provide jobs but to make profits, beyond a certain point the customer base dwindles and the disaffected create harmful and costly disruptions. These outcomes must be avoided.

- To diminish the risks of civilisational clash, huge disparities now prevailing between wages for similar work at similar productivity levels in different parts of the world must be significantly reduced.

- The younger generation must be consciously socialised in the free-market culture; for the brightest, this initiation should include education for high future productivity. Entry-level jobs consonant with that education must be plentiful. Unskilled labourers' jobs for the less bright must remain available.

- Many of these jobs can be provided in the domain of ecological renewal. Destruction of the environmental substratum must cease. The market itself must take the lead in an ecological revolution or risk losing its physical base. Supplies of food, water and energy in particular must remain adequate and reasonably priced.

- The state must concentrate on the provision of basic infrastructure and physical security to its citizens. It should be as little involved as possible in management or regulatory functions. At present, because it is obliged to keep a wide variety of imminent crises under control, the state has exceeded its proper limits.

- Although intragovernmental public institutions must continue to play a role, international regulation can be best accomplished through new institutions serving the interests of private enterprise. Sooner rather than later, the world will require global institutions which can make rapid executive decisions, a task for which the present United Nations is totally inadequate.

- As affluent citizens participate increasingly in financial markets, they should be able to purchase 'anti-crash' insurance with guarantees constituted by their premiums, augmented by a small international tax on financial transactions to be administered by a consortium of international reinsurers.

- Religions and religious expression must be forced to confine themselves to their proper sphere.

- The spread of the illegal economy, including the traffic in illegal aliens, must be halted; if governments are not equal to this task it must be undertaken by private enterprise.

These are merely minimum, not exhaustive, conditions for the continuing success of global capitalism. Even so, *none of them can be satisfied under present demographic circumstances*. Their fulfilment is totally incompatible with a human population of 6 billion or more.

Let us assume, however, that it were decided that 'we' could support 8 to 12 billion people. What sort of people would they be? What would supporting them require? To begin with, since there would be far more Outs than Ins, it would dictate an unending transfer from wealth creators to wealth consumers. Those who did not (and doubtless could not) contribute anything to the system would still expect it to service their needs. Hundreds of millions could not be absorbed into the productive economy yet would demand some version of a universal welfare state to take care of them.

Either they would already be massively present inside the productive countries or they would have to be paid not to go there. Wherever they were, their presence would be accompanied by the paraphernalia of a vast administrative bureaucracy. National and international taxation of all income-earning, productive individuals and profitable firms would reach astronomical levels. When the productive and the unproductive clashed, just as bad money drives out good, so the low living standards of the losers would drive out the higher living standards of the winners.

To sustain such numbers, we would also need a global environmental police force and a strict judicial system to make sure that drastic conservation measures were instituted and obeyed. Even so, with 8 to 12 billion people on earth, we could not prevent massive deforestation, species habitat destruction, mushrooming, unliveable and polluted cities, lakes and seas dead from industrial and human wastes; all constantly intensified by ever-growing multitudes, until the entire substance of the earth was devastated and consumed.

Income transfers from the relatively rich to the absolutely poor would necessarily be accompanied by transfers of power; the West would have to relinquish not just its wealth but its authority. It would thereby seal the fate of the liberal system and ensure its certain demise. The entire exercise would be revealed as self-defeating.

The Commissioning Parties have instructed us to be straightforward and explicit. They will have drawn for themselves the unmistakable conclusions of our analysis: we cannot both sustain the liberal, free-market system and simultaneously continue to tolerate the presence of superfluous billions.

The original meaning of 'proletarian', *proletarius*, is 'one who serves the state not with property but with offspring'. The state, like the world at large, is today dis-served in this manner. Today's *proletarius* serves only himself by having offspring; indeed, within his social stratum, the lifelong and measurable transfer of wealth flows from children to parents, not, as in mature and modern societies, from parents to children. He has many incentives to continue to reproduce. His offspring will produce more offspring, continuing the cycle of proliferation, dis-service to the state and, ultimately, destruction of the local, national and global communities.

Those unfit to participate in the system because they are unable or unwilling to embrace its culture now place far too high a burden on the system and weigh upon it far too heavily. They can only constitute a drain on the mass of productive individuals. The latter will eventually refuse to support the huge and growing numbers of the unproductive, even at present inadequate (as seen from the point of view of the unproductive) levels. Clash is inevitable, not just between civilisations, but within all our present social spaces.

The only way to guarantee the happiness and well-being of the vast majority is for the total population of the earth to be proportionally smaller. This choice may appear stark but it is dictated at once by reason and by compassion. If we wish to preserve the liberal system – the very premise of our assignment – there is no alternative. All else is illusion and wishful thinking.

We believe this course to be not only economically, socially and ecologically imperative but ethically defensible. Fewer people living in a less stressed environment would mean that all were better off. Instead of continually depressed living standards and the reign of anarchy, the rule of law would prevail, the pursuit of happiness could become a reality, the planet would survive. Such is the true meaning of the slogan 'sustainable development'. It is upon this foundation that Part Two of our Report is based.

Part Two

2.1

Goals

'God moves in a mysterious way, his wonders to perform', declares the eighteenth-century poet Cowper in 'Light Shining out of Darkness'. God's ways may seem severe, even cruel, yet for our own happiness we should accept whatever trials He chooses for us. 'The bud may have a bitter taste, but sweet will be the flower.' The poet's faith in Divine Providence resembles the trust placed by *laissez-faire* in the Invisible Hand.

Our intent is not to shock or blaspheme: the fact remains that in earthly affairs, the market, at its broadest and most inclusive, is the closest we are likely to come to the wisdom of the Almighty. Yes, the market creates suffering for some; its decisions may appear harsh and cruel, but let us not forget the theological parallel to the market according to which 'God, supremely good, would never allow that there be evil in His works unless He were so powerful and so good that even from evil He could do good.'[1]

If capitalism can be said to possess an ontology, an essence, it is surely that the market, in its full sweep and scope, is harmonious and wise. Like God, it too can create good from apparent evil. From destruction it draws the betterment of humankind and the highest possible equilibrium of the whole.

The moment has come to put this ontology to the test. It is time to ask if the beneficiaries of the free-market and the liberal system, including the Commissioning Parties, are prepared to accept the seemingly harsh consequences of their beliefs.

Can the environment and civilised society sustain present and future numbers? Should Western culture be represented by 15, then 10, then 5 per cent of humanity? Should the most productive individuals and nations sacrifice their well-being in the name of problematic gains for the least productive ones? Should now-powerful countries willingly relinquish their authority? Such are the questions our analysis obliges us to put to ourselves and to the Commissioning Parties; for our part, we answer 'no' to all of them.

We have dwelt at length on the likelihood of environmental collapse and social anarchy. We have spoken of the mirage of the universal welfare state and the illusion of universal human inclusion. We have warned against the folly of renouncing one's own power and culture in the bargain. As Machiavelli pointed out to the Medici long ago, the choice is to remain Prince and to do whatever is necessary to that end, or to cease to be Prince. We have no doubt that the Commissioning Parties will choose to remain, as it were, Prince. The great question thus becomes, 'What is necessary to that end?'

Mistaken Strategies

If twenty-first century capitalism cannot continue to function optimally – if at all – under foreseeable future demographic conditions, then those conditions must be altered.

Such a statement, should it be seized upon by self-appointed moralists, would doubtless be denounced as a declaration of intended 'genocide'. Not only would this betray a careless use of language; it is not what we intend.

'Genocide' stems from the Greek *genos*, meaning 'race' or 'kind'; it means the systematic extermination of the members of a particular ethnic or linguistic group. History has extended this definition to extermination based on religion, culture, political persuasion and, in at least one case, sexual orientation.

Our century has witnessed spectacular genocides. Time after time, powerful fanatics have forced huge numbers of their contemporaries to submit to their views of racial or political purity. The Nazis placed race and their hatred of Jews at the centre of their creed, though they also found time for gypsies, communists and homosexuals.

Class domination ('the dictatorship of the proletariat') lay at the theoretical heart of Stalinism and the Gulag. In the Great Leap Forward and the Cultural Revolution, Maoists sought forced industrialisation plus purity and uniformity of 'correct' political thought. The Khmer Rouge wanted a fundamentalist agrarianism from which intellectuals would be banished. The Indonesians eliminated communists and East Timorese in the name of nationalism. In overcrowded Rwanda, the Hutus appealed to ethnicity in order to take over the land and resources of the rival Tutsis.

All these genocidal systems were based on discrimination and in the case of the most sophisticated ones, like the Nazis or the Stalinists, on a vast administrative bureaucracy underpinning a complex eradication machine. Yet all were primitive, provincial and inept:

- They were costly in terms of time, personnel, money and material. One could argue that, fortunately for the rest of us, the Nazis lost the war because they diverted too many vital resources to exterminating Jews and were brought down by their racialist obsessions.

- They were inefficient. The burden of victim selection fell upon the state machinery which inevitably (through corruption, individual choices, poor timing, bureaucratic snafus or what have you) created multiple avenues of escape.

- They conferred far too much power and responsibility on the state because they required a massive state apparatus and by themselves virtually justified its existence.

- They were highly visible. Despite widespread voluntary blindness and solemn protestations of ignorance on the part of both locals and foreigners, these genocidal enterprises were well known as they occurred. After the fact they became universally known.

- They brought ruin and opprobrium to those who perpetrated them. Subordinates, bystanders and all those connected at any level with the genocidal enterprise were targeted as criminals and moral outcasts.

- They failed utterly. Do Jews have their own state today? Are they for the most part successful, in many countries, occupying positions of prestige and responsibility in numerous fields of public and private endeavour? Are Stalinists now in power anywhere (with the possible exceptions of North Korea and Cuba)? Does the USSR even exist? To ask these questions is to answer them. Neither the Holocaust nor the Gulag (the Cultural Revolution, the Khmer Rouge, and so on) succeeded, even *on its own terms*.

A Different Drummer

None of this is what we have in mind. To begin with, we are not ideologically motivated and we harbour no hatred for any ethnic group, religion or race. Such sentiments are puerile and unworthy. Secondly, we are not speaking here about some lunatic utopia ('the world will be perfect when all Jews/class enemies have been eliminated and the people/party purified'). Our goals are rather to:

- create an economic environment which will maximise individual chances for success and the pursuit of happiness;

- safeguard a liveable habitat for humans and other species;

- perpetuate civilised society and Western culture.

The first goal – to create a favourable economic environment – requires that we first determine *under what conditions* it is possible to ensure not some ultimate, ideal system but the greatest possible welfare for the greatest possible number. If the free market does not provide for 'pursuing happiness' more readily than some other alternative system, it deserves to lose its pre-eminent place. A system based upon competition should not fear it!

The liberal, market-based system does not now provide happiness, comfort and a measure of security for the majority of humanity; nor will it do so for projected populations in future: these are givens and must be recognised. We doubt that any other system could do so either, but in the context of this Report that is irrelevant. Even in the best-off countries, not everyone can possess and accumulate capital or succeed as a risk-taking entrepreneur; whereas the labour market is just that, a market, obeying market rules.

According to the founding principle of competition, the global market takes the best and leaves the rest. Today, although no one knows for sure, the 'rest' are almost certainly more numerous than those whose talents, skills, education, moral qualities, birth, luck and so on have placed them inside the system. Even the International Labour Organisation puts the numbers of those 'unincorporated' in the labour force at over a billion: add their dependants and the enormous size of this category becomes apparent.

Our second goal – safeguarding a liveable habitat – is curiously akin to the views expressed by the so-called 'Deep Ecology' movement. Although we are far from subscribing to all its premises, we note with interest the following statements from its *Platform*:

> The flourishing of human life and cultures is *compatible with a substantial decrease of the human population*. The flourishing of non-human life *requires such a decrease*. Policies must therefore be changed.[2] [our emphasis]

The Deep Ecologists do not say how or by whom the 'substantial decrease' might be achieved, nor which policies would have to be changed to achieve it. They simply state the obvious. To our knowledge, Deep Ecologists are not being held in custody for advocating 'genocide'.

Our third goal – perpetuating civilised society and Western culture – cannot be attained today in the same ways as it has been during most of recorded history. For centuries, politics and war were concerned with gaining control over *greater* numbers of people. Integrating large foreign populations into one's *imperium* did not threaten civilised society, quite the contrary. Although Barbarian or Mongol hordes may have been interested solely in rape and pillage and although a city might have to be destroyed in order to hold it, the best strategy was 'to allow the conquered to continue to live under their own laws, subject to a regular tribute, and to create in them a government of a few who will keep the country friendly to the conqueror'.[3]

From the time of the Greeks and the Romans to that of the nineteenth-century colonists, sophisticated conquerors always sought to incorporate the land, resources, wealth *and people* of the conquered territory because they represented significant assets. The labour of the conquered population, often under the watchful eye and the heavy rod of a collaborating local oligarchy, was another source of riches and power. Today, the idea of holding colonies is faintly ludicrous: their assets can be better extracted through other methods, their populations are, for the most part, not merely useless but burdensome as well.

The Enclosure Movement in Britain was a harbinger of things to come, dispossessing thousands of small farmers and creating a floating population. However, until the machines of the Industrial Revolution put masses of traditional craftsmen out of work, the problem of excess populations never arose.

Until our own day, society could also count on various safety valves, first among them the celebrated Malthusian 'checks' like famines. Surplus labour and social misfits could also emigrate to the new lands opening in North America and Australia. Fifty million Europeans did so in the nineteenth century. Colonies elsewhere, particularly in Africa and the Indian subcontinent, helped to take up the slack as well.

Armies conscripted and disciplined many otherwise anti-social youth. Families were expected to care for indigent members. Organised charity developed at the same time as the Industrial Revolution itself and dealt with many of its unsavoury consequences.

We no longer enjoy these luxuries. The world is full and there are no empty spaces left to settle or colonise. Armed forces are on the whole professionalised and no longer perform their disciplinary mission towards conscripts. In the North, families are nuclear, lack living space and have no time to care for poor, sick or aged relatives. The notion that private charity or even public aid can deal with the full range of present social ills is absurd.

Just as physical rubbish and waste litter the landscape and threaten to overwhelm many cities and their services, so social rubbish and waste endanger liberal ideals and the market, though few dare to say so in public. Proper management and social control are impossible when all efforts to ameliorate the situation are immediately neutralised, indeed swamped by proliferating, poorly integrated populations.

The question for us is therefore not *whether* but *how* to achieve the goal of drastic population reduction. In this regard, we wish to state firstly some general principles, referring explicitly and in the same sequence to the errors of those earlier ('genocidal') methods we identified above and which we called 'primitive, provincial and inept'.

- Although not entirely cost-free, modern population reduction strategies must be cheap, requiring no special equipment and virtually no manpower. The 'Auschwitz model' is the opposite of what is required to attain the objective. It is also far more important to redirect spending than to raise new funds.

- 'Victim' selection should not be undertaken by anyone but the 'victims' themselves. They will self-select on criteria of incompetence, inaptitude, poverty, ignorance, laziness, criminality and the like; in a word, 'loser-hood'.

- The state should have relatively few duties to perform with regard to population management and in any case far fewer tasks than those connected with vast prison administrations, unemployment compensation, overall 'welfare' administration and the like. We advocate downgrading the present size and scope of the state and reducing significantly its role in people's affairs. We are thus consistent in recommending that the state take its cue from the private sector in the area of population control as well.

- In the matter of visibility and public perceptions, we recommend two categories of strategies. 'Preventive' population control will centre on birth prevention, it will be visible and part of normal policy; whereas 'curative' strategies will deal with those already born but will not appear to have any particular agency behind them. There are no villains in this scenario.

- As a consequence, the question of opprobrium should not arise.

- Properly thought through, with sufficient moral energy and financial commitment behind them, these strategies, taken together, could succeed. The task of the Working Party is to think them through; the energy and commitment must be supplied by the Commissioning Parties and their allies.

The twenty-first century must choose between discipline and control or tumult and chaos. The only way to ensure the greatest welfare for the greatest number while still preserving capitalism is to make that number smaller. We have arrived at this conclusion after carefully weighing the alternatives. If no action is taken, some future Working Party may still debate whether social anarchy will precede, follow or accompany ecological collapse, but the basic questions will have been settled negatively for civilisation. We ask the Commissioning Parties to appreciate that our message is not merely that 'the ends justify the means', though this may well be so. It is, rather, that Western culture and the liberal market system must, in the twenty-first century, choose between the ends and The End.

Present Populations and Targets for Tomorrow

The first objective is to determine the optimum population level in the next century, allowing the smoothest possible functioning of the global market economy while ensuring ecological and social harmony and well-being for the great majority.

Depending on the set of 'low, medium, high or constant fertility' assumptions chosen, the United Nations estimates that in 2020 world population will be somewhere between 7.2 and 8.5 billion. Since fertility does indeed seem to be declining nearly everywhere, we will discount the 'constant fertility' scenario whose numerical outcome would be 8.5 billion people in 2020. The UN's 'low' case, however, which comes out at 7.2 billion, errs too much on the downside, assuming that within two decades, birth rates in poor countries will have dropped, voluntarily, by nearly 40 per cent compared to those of today!

As noted, the UN claims that about 81 million people are now added annually to world population (roughly 133 million births and 52 million deaths). In more immediately apprehended terms, this means that some 15,000 babies are born every hour or 250 a minute. Deaths, in contrast, are 6,000 an hour or 100 a minute.

We have noted too that many experts urge scepticism with regard to UN figures and caution that it consistently underestimates world population because it is obliged to trust (and print) what governments tell it. In their view, present population increases are 90 to 100 million per year.

We cannot settle the matter of annual additional numbers definitively (nor can anyone else) but we have chosen to base our own calculations on the UN's 'high' case projections as probably closest to the truth. These projections foresee 8 billion people in the year 2020.

Table I

Population (millions) and % of total	1995 (UN estimate)	2020 (UN 'high' estimate)	Difference 1995–2020
World	5687 (100%)	8062 (100%)	+2375 (+42%)
More developed regions	1171 (20.6%)	1267 (15.7%)	+ 96 (+0.08%)
Less developed regions	4516 (79.4%)	6794 (84.3%)	+2278 (+50%)

Source: United Nations Population Division *World Population Prospects: The 1996 Revision* (Statistical Annexes, Various Tables), 24 October 1996.

In this soon-to-be world of 8 billion people, if nothing interferes with present trends, in 2020 the population of the less developed regions will be nearly 7 billion, up 50 per cent from 1995. These regions will represent 84 per cent of humanity as compared to 79 per cent today. In contrast, the population of the developed regions will have increased only imperceptibly.

The internal dynamics of the more and less developed worlds will be completely at odds as well. For one thing, population density in the rich world will average 23 people per square kilometre in 2020, virtually unchanged from 20 in 1975, 22 in 1995. The poor world, in contrast, will witness in 2020 an average 78 people per square kilometre (up from 37 in 1975, 55 in 1995). Naturally, huge variations in densities exist in both regions – from 4 in Canada and 24 in Brazil to 387 in India, 396 in the Netherlands and 524 in Korea. But only a small part of the land anywhere is fertile. Overcrowding and environmental degradation in much of the South is spiralling. People will necessarily seek to escape.

Age structures will also have a profound influence.

The figures in Table II are redolent of future conflicts. In the rich world in the year 2020, nearly one-quarter of the population will be over 60 (including 18 per cent, that is nearly one person in five, over 65). Much political power will be concentrated in the hands of the relatively elderly.

Table II

Area	World %		More developed regions %		Less developed regions %	
Age group	1995	2020	1995	2020	1995	2020
0–14	31.4	27.7	18.6	18.6	34.4	29.4
15–24	18	16	14	11.7	19.1	17
25–59	41	43	49	45.5	39.2	43.3
60+	9.5	12.5	18.3	24.2	7.3	10.3

Source: United Nations Population Division *World Population Prospects: The 1996 Revision* (Statistical Annexes, Various Tables), 24 October 1996.

Those in their most productive years, between the ages of 24 and 59, will number well under half of the inhabitants of these developed countries. Yet they will be bringing up the same percentage of young children as in 1995, while struggling to educate older ones through the longer higher studies indispensable for success in a globalised, competitive world. At the same time, they will be obliged to care for (or pay for the care of) ageing parents. The median age in the rich world will be 41. Between parents, children and ever-more demanding jobs, these people will be under constant stress and are unlikely to have much patience or sympathy with calls for help emanating from the other 84 per cent of humanity.

In the poor world, where well over half the population today is under 24 years old, the proportion of young people will have dwindled slightly by the year 2020, down to 46 per cent. Forty-three per cent will be in their middle, most productive years. Although they will still have a lot of children to raise, they will not be burdened with many elders: only 10 per cent in the less developed world will be over 60, and just 6.8 per cent – almost three times less than in the richer world – will be over 65.

In this poorer, less educated world, the untrammelled energies of the young are slated to prevail: the median age will be 27 (as opposed to 24 today). They will expect their demands to be heard by their own governments and by the world at large. These facts and figures all point towards the same goal: in our considered view, *the target for 2020 should be to cut present numbers by a third, from roughly 6 billion to 4. Put another way, one should seek to cut by one half the current UN 'high variant' estimate of 8 billion people in 2020.*

This is why, in the latter stages of preparing this Report, we adopted the shorthand *2020 –2: Twenty-twenty Minus Two*, since the starting point today is about 6 billion. We might as easily have said Twenty-twenty divided by two. Whatever the formula, the effort to be undertaken is monumental.

This goal represents a return to 1975, when world population was 4 billion, one-quarter of it in the developed world, three-quarters in the developing (as one then called them) areas. It was a time of relative peace and prosperity: the trauma of the Vietnam War was over, the less developed countries were looking to the future with optimism and ordinary people in the developed countries were enjoying unprecedented gains. The environment had not yet registered the terrible shocks from which it now suffers. In a word, the world may not have been perfect but it was manageable.

To make it manageable again, the curve in Figure 1 expresses the ideal scenario and it requires that preparations for implementing the recommendations made hereunder begin immediately. We begin with 6 billion human units in the year 2000 with the goal of attaining 4 billion within 20 years. Although the curve would initially continue to increase, in the final stage there would be an annual decline of up to 280 million net units. In terms of timelines, around the year 2005, world population would attain its maximum value of 6.4 billion. Five years later, in 2010, it would have settled back to today's level of about 6 billion. For the next ten years, until 2020, absolute and quite rapid decline would ensue.

Where should the reductions take place? At present, the developed world 'contributes' less than 10 per cent of world births and 23 per cent of world deaths. Thus of the 81 million people added annually to world population (still accepting the UN figures) only 1 million people net are added in the richer countries. In rare cases, as in Germany, the native population is actually in decline. Any population growth can be attributed solely to births within immigrant communities.

The figure to focus on is the 81 million added, net, each year to world population in the poor world, according to conserva-

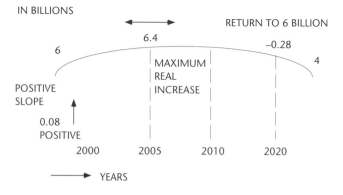

Figure 1 Ideal Population Scenario[4]

tive estimates. If nothing changes, these 81 million will become 90 million by 2005 and 100 million in 2020. If the UN's figures are already too low at 80 million today, one can see the staggering numbers we can expect in 2020 – if nothing changes.

To reach the target of 4 billion in 2020, world population must be reduced on average by 100 million people a year for two decades. Nine-tenths or more of the reduction should take place in the less developed countries. Effort must be brought to bear both on mortality increase and fertility decrease in proportions which will vary according to time and chance.

For obvious reasons, we can provide only guidelines, not mathematical certainties. Many factors involved are beyond anyone's control: both obstacles and opportunities will arise unexpectedly. We recognise that the task is herculean but this is no excuse not to undertake it. If it is to be accomplished, it will require all the energies and the means that the Commissioning Parties can command.

2.2

Pillars

We are not engineers nor do we possess technical expertise in all the fields to be covered; thus we do not pretend to provide blueprints or 'nuts-and-bolts' solutions. We can, however, supply a general framework for posing the important strategic questions and point to areas in which technical expertise might usefully be recruited.

Before describing 'preventive' and 'curative' strategies, we find it important to highlight current trends which should be encouraged or discouraged so as to perpetuate capitalism, the only system we believe capable of ensuring the greatest good of the greatest number. The first step is to consolidate the foundations for the ambitious undertaking of massive population reduction. These foundations have four pillars:

- ideological-ethical

- economic

- political

- psychological

Although they should remain hidden from view, these pillars undergird the visible strategic edifice. They are also, in the full architectural sense, mutually reinforcing.

The Ideological-Ethical Pillar

Why be concerned with ideas and beliefs rather than proceeding immediately to practical matters? Simply because ideas and beliefs govern the world – but they are not immutable. They emerge and are shaped according to the needs of the times; Marx would have said that they evolve to suit the needs of the dominant classes. Ideology is water for the fish of which the fish are unaware. Our concern here is to mould ideology consciously so that the dominant ideas and beliefs of our time serve to justify the grand design.

For example, our era looks on epidemics or famines anywhere on the planet with horror, yet the early Christian theologian Tertullian wrote of 'the scourges of pestilence, famine, wars and earthquakes [which] *have come to be regarded as a blessing* to overcrowded nations, since they serve to prune away the luxuriant growth of the human race'. He lamented as well the 'vast population of the earth to which we are a burden', to the point that 'she scarcely can provide for our needs'.[1]

For this Church father, natural or man-made scourges are positive 'blessings' because they save 'overcrowded nations' from the dire consequences of their own reproduction. War, famine and pestilence safeguard the community and the future. Thanks to these so-called calamities, in reality beneficial to humanity, the survivors and their descendants will once more enjoy earth's bounty. Without them, the earth could never 'provide for our needs', all the more because these needs are growing all the time.

Christian that he was, this theologian did not see individual life as the highest good. He placed, rather, the common welfare at the apex of his scale of values and recognised that some branches of mankind's family tree must be pruned and its 'luxuriant growth' tamed to insure that collective welfare prevailed. We have already cited the views of classical philosophers like Plato and Aristotle who correctly saw overpopulation as a grave danger to the community and the state.

Our own age and its ideology belong instead to the individual. The market mechanism and liberalism itself are based on the private decisions and risks freely taken by countless individuals. Similarly, our dominant ethics and our systems of law deal only with individual (or 'human') rights, conscience and actions; our justice with individual crimes and misdeeds. We have consequently lost touch with the notions of collective offence and the greatest good of the whole. This good may sometimes necessitate coercion and sacrifices which our era no longer recognises as legally or morally justifiable. Our societies are hard put to apply the concept of collective responsibility, much less that of collective guilt for the state of the common weal.

The proof is that we still consider it 'ethically correct' that illiterate, unemployable, superfluous, degenerate people continue to proliferate and to propagate as much as they like; to the point that judgements such as this one cannot even be expressed in public without immediate censure, pious denunciations and, in certain contexts, legal action. Plato, Aristotle and Tertullian would have been dismayed by this state of affairs, just as they would have been astonished by the Universal Declaration of Human Rights!

If the ground rules are to be changed and the strategy we recommend is to succeed, it is imperative that we first transform the current ideological climate and put our conceptual and ethical houses in order. Dominant ethical systems have evolved throughout history and there is no reason why they cannot change again. If ethics can be seen as a given society's collective survival strategy, ours is in need of serious overhaul. Our present ethics will reject effective population management unless and until the contradictions between market individualism, 'human rights' and the need for collective harmony are resolved.

The initial step is to recognise and cause others to recognise dispassionately that a vigorous, competitive and globalised economy will necessarily create a two-tier society of winners and losers, Ins and Outs, both within countries and between them. This is healthy. It is the mainspring of the system, the 'nature of the beast' and in any case cannot be altered.

Rather than attempting vainly to change this nature, one must seek to maximise the winners, minimise the losers and confer on a far larger proportion of humanity than today the advantages the market can procure. Far more people must be incorporated in both North and South; one must also ensure a social environment in which the major ills of rich societies (crime, unemployment, pollution, addiction and the like) have visibly diminished.

It is plain that the market, on its own, cannot create mass welfare under present demographic conditions and that these must consequently be corrected. For genuine population control to become acceptable, a new climate of thought and opinion must be instituted; one which *does not assume doctrinaire and unlimited personal freedom as its starting point nor 'human rights' as its fulcrum.*

We therefore strongly encourage the Commissioning Parties to create and sustain a body of thinkers, writers, teachers and communicators who can develop concepts, arguments and images providing intellectual, moral, economic, political and psychological justification for vigorous population management strategies. These intellectual workers should also elaborate and convey an innovative and practical twenty-first-century ethics.

A substantial investment in the proper ideological framework would repay itself a hundredfold. The ideas of great thinkers like Plato, Darwin, Hobbes, Malthus, Nietzsche, Hayek, Nozick (and we would audaciously hope the ideas and arguments contained in this Report as well) should be dusted off where necessary, fine-tuned, adapted to the *goût du jour*, repackaged for different audiences and disseminated among opinion-shapers, decision-makers and the general public.

The findings of modern bioscience, ecology, demography, sociology, neo-classical economics and other disciplines, judiciously interpreted, will naturally find their place in the structures of a renovated intellectual edifice. These ideas must be elaborated, shaped and promoted through a network, a committed intellectual cadre, whose members should receive generous stipends and the physical and mental space in which to work and develop their ideas, whether in traditional universities, specialised foundations and institutes or through cyber-networks.

They must have access not merely to publication in books and journals but also to the mainstream press, radio, television and electronic media. They should be given ample opportunity to speak at public and private functions, to encounter and instruct the young, to develop multiple websites.

Without self-conscious and dynamic intellectual leadership, authority and justification, we warn that the strategies outlined in this Report are destined to fail. We assume that the creation, maintenance and promotion of such a corps of 'ideological legionnaires' should present few problems to the Commissioning Parties. They are also doubtless acquainted with the leadership of the growing globalised media conglomerates whose assets include all the requisite 'intellectual-ideological amplifiers' for the dissemination of ideas.[2]

In all candour, Working Party members think of themselves as a kind of prototype for this intellectual cadre. In addition, they freely admit to having been attracted by the material rewards of their participation in this enterprise, above and beyond its intrinsic merits. We are no different in this respect from other professional thinkers, scientists and writers who will recognise the manifest advantages of liberalism and place their knowledge and talents in the service of the free market when it is clearly profitable and beneficial for them to do so.

Yet we must introduce here a further note of caution. Even if the ideological work is brilliantly carried out by a cadre of genius with generous financial and technological means at its disposal, it will still fail if the system cannot truly deliver an ever-greater measure of economic well-being, ecological renewal and civilisational values to the majority of earth's inhabitants. If it is found wanting, the Outs will sooner or later revolt and bring liberal capitalism crashing down with them.

The Economic Pillar

This is why certain economic policies must be instituted or reinforced without delay. Up to now, structural adjustment programmes (SAPs) put in place by the World Bank and the International Monetary Fund in countries of the South and the East have been the norm. They have undeniably played a positive role. They introduce no-nonsense neo-liberal discipline, oblige governments to integrate their national economies into the global one and provide a framework in which local elites can enrich themselves (through lower wages, a more docile workforce, massive privatisation, less government intervention, and so on). This elite-orientation of SAPs serves to create influential national stakeholders and investors in neo-liberalism and globalisation.

Although it may be difficult to prove, SAPs have probably dampened population growth even though they have not reduced total populations. The time has come to link specifically economic and demographic goals. The opportunity to extend and reinforce SAPs exists since virtually all the countries concerned are far more indebted now than they were when they first undertook these programmes. Their indebtedness leaves them open to increasingly drastic IMF measures since they cannot obtain credit anywhere without the Fund's seal of approval. Now that all the populous nations of Asia, with the sole, though significant, exception of China, have been brought under IMF tutelage, genuine strides can be made.

SAPs can have a direct or indirect demographic effect. They are models of synergism. For example, they encourage agricultural production for export and raise food prices, thus depressing food intake and resistance to disease. Women may become prostitutes to make ends meet, then contract and spread AIDS. Public health budgets and funds for drainage or refuse collection are often slashed, with the consequence that malaria and other diseases return. Low wages result in lack of access to paid health care or medicines.

Wherever markets are rapidly liberalised, under duress or not, a favourable terrain for increased mortality and decreased fertility is created. In some places, life expectancies have already dropped dramatically, as in the former Soviet Union where employment and social services have undergone sharp cuts and five years have been pruned from the average lifespan. UNICEF claimed a decade ago that debt plus SAPs were causing the deaths of an additional half a million children a year, although this figure cannot be verified.

Western countries have a strong majority on the IMF Board and should see to it that structural adjustment programmes are reinforced. Unlike the World Bank, the Fund has never stooped to crowd-pleasing 'public relations' and we suggest that the conclusions of this Report might usefully be shared with judiciously selected senior Fund managers who would be sympathetic to its concerns.

Private financial capital can also play a positive role in creating favourable conditions for population curtailment. As opposed to investments in plant and equipment, purchases of stocks and bonds are fully liquid and can be withdrawn instantly. When the Mexican meltdown occurred in late 1994, the resulting peso crisis precipitated widespread business failures, skyrocketing interest rates, mass bankruptcies and dismissals of personnel. As a result, food consumption was cut by a quarter, suicide rates reached new highs and violent crimes became far more prevalent. A similar scenario already exists in

Russia and is now taking hold in Thailand, Korea, Indonesia and elsewhere in South-East Asia as well. Markets discipline instantly; they hold, as it were, permanent elections.

These public or private financial measures, properly managed, can lead to population curbs and support 'pruning' strategies. But whatever the advantages of adjustment or of volatile portfolio investment, they cannot do the whole job themselves. They must be accompanied by a refashioned political order in the service of the new world economic order.

The Political Pillar

Structural adjustment, however useful, is necessarily an attribute of the nation-state system in which individual governments, even under the tutelage of the IMF and the World Bank, remain the relevant entity and the reference point. To date, states have cooperated to a greater or lesser extent with liberalisation programmes. Smaller, weaker nations may have no choice; others have tried to rebel outright against drastic economic discipline. The picture is not uniform and much may depend on the ideological persuasion of the leadership. The fact remains that in many countries, adjustment has failed.

This is not the fault of the Fund or the Bank. They have done outstanding, pioneering work but they have also been obliged to function in a shaky and ambiguous political framework. Their own legitimacy has been questioned, not only by popular organisations but also by governments. Existing world political authorities cannot dictate adequate rules to solve the obvious problems of today and are grossly inadequate if population pruning strategies are to become operational tomorrow.

The objective must now be to replace the outdated nation-state model. The late twentieth century has witnessed the near-triumph of economic globalisation; the task of the twenty-first century will be to create the legitimate, universally recognised global political structure to support, sustain and perfect it. Whatever its shortcomings, a rejuvenated IMF will probably be a vital part of this framework. It should use each successive financial crisis to enhance its doctrinal authority and its coercive power.

A trailblazer, as noted, is the innovative – indeed revolutionary – World Trade Organisation (WTO). For the first time, an international body enjoys genuine judicial power over trade disputes with regard to all its member states rich or poor, large or small, weak or powerful.

Another positive element of this work-in-progress is the Multilateral Agreement on Investment (MAI), under negotiation as we convene. The MAI could add teeth to world economic governance by creating a coercive transnational framework for private corporate investment, superseding national laws.

The MAI should be given real teeth and ratified as soon as possible. As one responsible official has said, 'Remember this is only the first step, like GATT in 1947. MAI is supposed to be the nucleus of a global economic constitution. We are entering a process of historic dimensions.' We hope he will be heard.

Taken together, and assuming consultation and cooperation between them, the IMF, the WTO and the MAI could function as an embryonic International Ministry of Finance, Investment and Trade. But this is indeed just a start. Clearly, they could not, by themselves, constitute a planetary government with universal powers of enforcement.

The threshold of the millennium is thus fraught with dangers. Nation-states have been unquestionably weakened, yet no genuine, recognised, supranational political power has yet been instated to replace them. How might this vacuum be filled?

- The global market should itself remain the chief organising principle of society. However, contrary to the views of some doctrinaire apologists, the market cannot be entirely self-regulating. It must be guided and channelled in order to safeguard its own future, and ours. This principle holds true particularly in the domain of financial markets. It may be too early to recommend a global currency, but it is certain that the paramount need is for a strong executive, able to move with speed and authority and to take and enforce decisions on economic and political matters of universal scope.

- This executive should take upon itself to regulate financial markets, perhaps through a much strengthened Bank for International Settlements. These markets should be taxed in order to provide revenues for the functioning of the executive.

- Transnational corporations should be deeply involved in designing the new political structures and will participate actively in their instatement, just as they have done within the WTO and the MAI. However, they must certainly not be seen to govern directly.

- The European Commission, formally representing governments but unaccountable in nearly all respects to the European Parliament, much less to national parliaments, may furnish an initial model of a transnational executive.

- The G-7 should explore a similar role. Already, meetings are not confined to G-7 heads of state but are convened for G-7 finance (or other) ministers as well. High level bureaucrats should be next, with specific mandates to develop collective decision-making machinery on sensitive subjects.

- Skilfully handled, the United Nations could be used to help constitute a world executive. If its proliferating agencies were restructured, merged and radically downsized, if the UN were prepared to model itself on the information-gathering and decision-making skills of private enterprise, it could contribute legitimacy to the process of international executive building. The present Secretary-General is clearly receptive to this message.

- Whereas a strong executive is a clear requirement, the world is now too complex to admit of international legislative bodies which are, in any case, territorially based. Parliamentary democracy should be seen as a 200-year parenthesis between different kinds of necessarily more authoritarian rule.

- Non-governmental organisations (NGOs) should, however, continue to be allowed 'consultative status' within a formal body sitting at regular intervals. Representatives in this permanent NGO forum could be elected or not, according to the policies of each member state. Successfully tested in the long string of UN conferences during the 1990s, this model has proven its capacity to make NGOs more 'constructive' and 'responsible', that is far less radical, challenging and unruly.

- The only traditional branch of government best left to the nation-state is the judiciary, including police jurisdiction, maintenance of local order, the court system, prisons and the like.

- Any political order requires a military enforcement mechanism. The Pentagon with the National Security Agency and an enlarged NATO seems destined to play such a role. It should maintain trustworthy second-tier military establishments in certain client states in the culturally diverse, non-Western civilisational areas.

- Information technologies will be paramount in the construction and consolidation of a renovated world order. Elites are already linked through dedicated networks and these links will necessarily be reinforced as the need for global political consultation and management becomes ever more apparent. Information technology will enhance surveillance, infiltration and disruption of nascent opposition.

'Citizenship' must be redefined (with the help of the ideological pillar, see above) and full use made of interactive, easily manipulated information networks to create the illusion of popular participation in decision-making. Once more, the tools of political control must remain largely invisible to those controlled, otherwise planetary management and even smooth market functioning will break down. The international scene will be rife with waste, confusion and anarchy.

The Psychological Pillar

The final pillar is closely related to the ideological-ethical matters discussed above. Individual and group psychologies, the 'battle for hearts and minds', nonetheless merit a place of their own. Properly channelled, they can help to create a favourable atmosphere for inter-group hostilities, themselves conducive to population reduction. Paradoxically, individual psychology can also enhance the spread of globalisation.

The most useful psychological tool yet forged for these purposes is 'identity politics' as it has come to be called in the West. Ideally, individuals everywhere should identify strongly with an ethnic, sexual, linguistic, racial, or religious sub-group to the detriment of self-definition as a national of any country or even as a member of a social class or professional caste of that nation, much less as part of the 'human race'. Each person should feel himself or herself to be *first* a member of a narrowly defined group and only secondarily a worker, a community member, a parent, a national or international citizen. The notion of 'citizenship', at any level, is to be actively discouraged.

Part of the ideological-ethical offensive outlined above should be devoted to providing material and moral support for the more articulate and aggressive spokespersons of sexual, racial, religious and ethnic particularisms. They should also have generous access to communications media with group-specific outlets established and financed wherever they do not occur spontaneously.

We are looking, as it were, for black, white, brown and yellow; gay, lesbian, feminist and phallocratic; Jewish, Christian, Hindu and Muslim fundamentalists and suprema-cists, as well as vulnerable and decried professional groups (from police to truck drivers), all with their own newspapers, maga-zines, radio, television and websites and all preoccupied above all else with their 'rights'. These rights should be conceived and ardently defended, not merely as negative (that is, the right to be free *from* harassment, violence or discrimination), but as affirmative (that is, the right to special treatment in the name of past or present, real or imaginary wrongs), up to and including the right to a separate state.

Since virtually every identifiable group on earth has been at some time or another, to a greater or lesser degree, a victim of some other group or simply of history and geography, the clam-ouring ought soon to become cacophonous and deafening, so that no other calls to arms can be heard above the din. The goal is to reinforce fragmentation, to underscore differences with others and to erect ghettos whether or not they have any basis in fact or tradition. Contrary to received opinion, most identi-ties, particularly the so-called 'ethnic' ones, have shallow historical roots and are more often than not of recent construc-tion. Identities are thus much like God: even if they do not exist, they are still extremely powerful – so much so that people will kill in their name.

The fastest way to create a strong and belligerent psychological sense of separateness is to make sure that a sufficient number of members of Group X are humiliated or killed by Group Y (or *believed* to be so humiliated or killed). Although such tensions are not always easy to create and to manipulate, the contemporary world offers many examples of doubtful ethnic and religious differences which have in this way been caused to surface and thrive. Enduring inter-group hatreds and ongoing conflicts can be served by the aggravation of existing racialist tendencies and by provocations guaranteed to make groups more receptive to violence.

Identity politics has two noteworthy advantages:

• First, it lays the groundwork for internal conflicts and civil wars by exacerbating all kinds of inter-communal tensions. Even when these tensions do not escalate as far as warfare, they keep high-profile groups angrily focused on each other and away from the real actors on the global stage who become virtually invisible.

• Second, it blocks solidarity and makes opposition to the strategies we recommend extremely problematic; rendering broad national or international fronts and alliances difficult if not impossible to establish, and preventing recourse to genuine politics.

Instead of asking themselves what they can *do*, people should be centred above all on who they *are*. Economic and political globalisation can proceed unimpeded so long as people are psychologically blindfolded and there is no corresponding global citizenry to oppose it.

One need only recall the Communist Manifesto's exhortation 'Workers of the world, Unite!' or the cry of the Parisian students and workers in May 1968, '*Nous sommes tous des juifs allemands*' ('We are all German Jews'), when the government tried to single out student leader Daniel Cohn-Bendit for special censure because of his religion and citizenship. The ideal situation is one in which future Cohn-Bendits feel *themselves* to be 'German Jews' (or whatever else) and apply themselves to tackling the problems of that specific group to the exclusion of others; whenever possible against other national, religious or ethnic groups.

Conversely, potential leaders who persist in strategies of solidarity and universality, like those who try to practise a citizen-based, inclusive nationalism should be personally discredited so that they will be mistrusted by their neighbours, students, workers, or colleagues, primarily on grounds of their race, ethnic origins, sexual preferences or financial probity.

Recent scientific work provides further insights into these matters and should be carefully followed as practical applications of the 'reduction imperative' proceed. In particular, game theory and primatology help to explain how and why humans cooperate and live in societies. Computer simulations of certain game strategies ('tit for tat', 'conditional cooperator', 'always defect', 'firm but fair', and so on) show that one can induce either conciliation and cooperation which continue indefinitely, or conversely, spiralling, inextricable mutual recriminations, hatred and 'blood feuds'. The construction of the psychological pillar will benefit from close study of these strategies and their outcomes.[3]

With these pillars now, we hope, firmly in place, we turn to the concrete elements of grand Population Reduction Strategy.

2.3

Scourges

Introduction

The Roman Empire reached its zenith in AD 200. when it counted 46 million subjects, including 28 million of the 36 million people then living in Europe. Italy was the most densely populated place in the Empire, with 19 persons per square kilometre (present population density in Italy is ten times that). Over the next four centuries, the population of Europe dropped by a quarter and it fell even more sharply in the Mediterranean countries. This dramatic decline was not caused by climate change, sweeping epidemic or any other identifiable single cause: according to two demographic historians, 'It looks very much as though classical society had simply over-expanded ...' Or, in more Malthusian terms, subsistence had simply failed to keep up with population.[1]

Whatever the causes, Roman civilisation did not survive long and soon gave way to the Dark Ages. Subsistence production stagnated and Europe's population only managed to claw its way back to the 36 million mark at the millennium. Between the years 1000 and 1300 there was a spurt of growth: by the beginning of the fourteenth century, Europe's population had reached an unprecedented 80 million.

It was too good to last. 'The Great Dying', as contemporaries called it, soon took care of at least one-quarter of them. The Black Death wiped out an even higher percentage in densely populated France, Italy and the Low Countries. Recovery was followed by another dip due to the devastation of the Thirty Years War.

Slowly, with the advent of the Industrial Revolution, improved diets and basic sanitation, in spite of wars, localised famine, disease and outmigration of 50 million souls, the European population shot up by 80 per cent from 1845 to 1914. The First World War brought down 8 million young men; even so, Europe's population grew by 40 per cent from 1914 to 1945. Since the Second World War it has stabilised and without immigrant populations from Turkey and North Africa it would probably be in overall decline.

China's demographic history is even more violent than Europe's. Its population peaked at around 50–60 million halfway through the Han Empire (206 BC–AD 220), then hovered there for another thousand years. Finally, improved rice cultivation techniques allowed it to provide for more mouths and the population prospered. China's plague was not Black but Mongol. The Khans, beginning with Genghis, massacred three-quarters of the inhabitants of the Northern provinces and one-third of those in the South – probably 35 million Chinese all told, a staggering number for the time. The population recovered, only to fall victim to the Manchus. They cut down 25 million Chinese in the seventeenth century and a further 25 million in the nineteenth. The Maoists with their Great Leap Forward clearly followed in some well-worn footsteps.

In other words, population reduction through conquest, war, famine or disease is nothing new. The difficulty is making it stick. In the course of developing and proposing our recommendations, we shall examine both preventive and curative Population Reduction Strategies, from now on frequently abbreviated to PRS. Preventive PRS centres on lower birth rates and curative PRS on higher death rates.

Although the *consequences* of curative strategies (increased mortality) may be more or less visible, we stress that there should not appear to be any specific agency behind them, unless it is fate and the manifold inadequacies of the victims themselves. The traditional scourges that once checked proliferating populations – war, famine, pestilence and earthquakes – are with us still, joined by more modern reinforcements like drugs, rampant crime and environmental poisons. We shall not deal with earthquakes or other acts of God which are beyond human powers to influence: if they occur they are bonuses, but should not be relied upon. As for the 'historical' scourges of conquest, war, famine and pestilence, the best guide remains Saint John, whose apocalyptic vision still blazes from the pages of *Revelation*, the final book of the Bible.

Precisely because John could not blame anyone in particular for the rampant scourges, he transformed them into metaphors and personified them in the Horsemen. (Conquest, it is true, has an agency. You can identify the perpetrator and, for whatever good it may do you, know you are being massacred by a Mongol or a Maoist.) The Four Horsemen will escort us as we continue on our journey in the realm of the 'How'. We must hope that the 'Why' has been established to the Commissioning Parties' satisfaction – for if not we shall have failed – and that they, too, are convinced of the need to 'prune away the luxuriant growth of the human race'.

The Apocalyptic Riders: A Contemporary Overview

I. Conquest

The First Horseman of the Apocalypse 'goes forth ... to conquer'. His horse is white and he carries a bow like the Parthians, imperial rivals and terror of the Roman world, masters of the famous over-the-shoulder 'Parthian shot'.

Dominion over others remains an important component of any Population Reduction Strategy. However, it can no longer be applied through Roman or Parthian methods of direct conquest, occupation and *imperium*. The usefulness of conquest, called colonisation in its most recent guise, has reached the end of the road because conquered territory and colonised peoples are no longer of any practical or material value.

Although it may have been important at one time for conquerors or colonists to provide for the upkeep of these peoples through food imports complementing erratic local production and by promoting public health policies, this is no longer the case. For at least two decades the need has been for fewer but more qualified workers. The resulting overpopulation with regard to the requirements of the world economy is not merely costly to the system but incompatible with traditional methods of political and social control.

This is why we have underscored instead the need for *non-traditional conquest* through ideological opinion moulding, ethical transformation and the creation of a new cultural hegemony in the Gramscian sense. We have also stressed indirect methods of dominion through reinforced structural adjustment, a severely weakened state and the constitution of a strong (though diffuse) and non-accountable international executive power working in close cooperation with transnational corporations. In order to diminish resistance to latter-day conquerors, we have also encouraged support for identity politics and the aggravation of ethnic and other communal tensions.

Wherever still useful territories and local activities exist, indirect conquest should prevail and mastery should remain invisible. We take as a counter-example the needlessly high profile of the Shell Oil Company in Nigeria where the Ogoni people have been certifiably poisoned and anti-Shell activists hanged in a travesty of justice.

Before his judicial murder in November 1995, the author Ken Saro-Wiwa wrote from his cell, 'Shell ... has exploited, traduced and driven the Ogoni people to extinction in the last three decades. The company has left a completely devastated environment and a trail of human misery. When I organised the Ogoni people to protest peacefully ... the company invited the Nigerian military to intervene ... I have one suggestion: boycott all Shell products.' Millions of people read and followed that suggestion or otherwise learned to associate 'Shell' with 'kangaroo court' and 'poison'. Shell should either have formed a local dummy company and bought off, employed and resettled the people or ceased activities harmful to its own reputation and to that of other transnational corporations.

We have scant sympathy with firms unwilling to make the slightest sacrifice for the greater good of the system in which they and others like them can flourish. We warn that unless the corporate world creates its own internal policing and enforcing authority empowered to deal with rogue TNCs and infringements of a written or unwritten code, it will sooner or later pay the price.

Brutality is stupid. The over-mastered should be unable to comprehend the organisation and methods of their masters and incapable of mobilising against them. The conqueror who acts at a great remove from the conquered cannot be targeted either through publicity, subversion or direct attack.

Our chief concern here is not, however, primarily with the power of the classical or modern conqueror to spare or to oppress individuals and societies but with the far more general notion of 'biopower' or 'biopolitics'. The late influential French scholar, Michel Foucault, originated this concept and analysed the historical transition between two quite different forms of rule.

Foucault differentiated between 'sovereignty' and 'biopower'. The first is recognised by its capacity to discipline, control, punish and if need be do away with individuals. The second takes the population in general as its object. 'Biopolitics' deals not with separate, identifiable people who have names and faces but with forecasts, statistics and global measures applied to the aggregate. It seeks therefore not to cure the illness or prolong the life of Peter, Paul or Mary but to improve life expectancy. To that end, it adopts a broad range of sanitary regulations; it tries to devise incentives for healthy behaviour and avoidance of accidents. These measures are aimed at the statistical entity called 'the population', not the individuals who compose it.

The transition from the rule of sovereignty to that of biopower occurred, according to Foucault, in the early nineteenth century and can be illustrated by attitudes towards death. In the earlier period, individual death was ritualised, subject to a ceremonial in which the whole family and often the whole group (clan, profession, court, and so on) participated. Under the biopolitical regime, death becomes intensely private, lonely, almost shameful, taboo. Death used to mark the moment when the individual ceased to be subject to the temporal sovereign and became the object of God's judgement. Biopower cares nothing about death: it deals only with mortality.

The technologies employed and institutions favoured by the two types of rule are also different. The sovereign's action is brought to bear on the individual body, rendering it disciplined, docile, useful. Biopower centres not on the body but on the mass, attempting to reduce the probability of various mishaps that can affect life in general. Sovereignty uses institutions like schools, hospitals, barracks and factories; biopower needs vast bureaucracies to administer social security and old-age pensions; to enforce rules of safety and hygiene. Births are medically attended, children are, by law, vaccinated, public housing sets standards, and so on.[2]

However useful Foucault's distinction, many of our institutions still lie somewhere between sovereignty and biopower. Medicine and hospitals deal with both the health of individual persons and that of the 'body politic'. Corporations still need to exercise control over the individual bodies of their employees but they do not do so by applying the old Henry Ford criteria of regularity and predictability to guarantee assembly line efficiency. Ford was a true 'sovereign' and his methods included intrusion by social workers into workers' private lives to search for unsatisfactory personal habits or home conditions that could make them ineligible for the full $5 daily wage.

Today's corporate organisation needs a less submissive, more flexible body. Some acknowledge this need explicitly through their training and retraining courses. 'Experiential training', to which many US corporations now have recourse, requires employees of both sexes, all ages and varying degrees of physical competence to scale high walls or wobbly poles, walk high wires, leap into space suspended from a zipline secured by a co-worker or stand on a foot-wide, rapidly swivelling platform before jumping into space again. This last exercise is termed the 'pamper pole' in honour of the well-known brand of nappies, because according to the training company, 'People so often defecate in their pants while trying to stand up on it.'

Those who survive these trials have learned viscerally that they must risk the unknown and tolerate fear yet recognise their dependency on the support of co-workers. Success in the age of rapid change and unprecedented competition will require 'letting go of old patterns and behaviours … taking a leap through difficult transitions and working hard at new beginnings'. Employees must learn to fit into a world which is no longer monolithic, hierarchical and bureaucratic but fleeting, fluid and flexible.[3]

We argue for our part that the world is entering an entirely new phase and that it is time to take Foucault's mid-1970s distinction a step further. A shift to power of a third kind, lying beyond sovereignty and biopower alike, is imperative. At first glance it might seem to lie in the hands of corporations; in fact it is centred in each individual's accountability to him or herself.

Under the new regime, at the individual level, people must take responsibility for, assume sovereignty over and indeed 'conquer' their own bodies if they expect to succeed and to survive in a competitive world. If they are not flexible in body, mind and spirit, they are dispensable and the world will quickly make them grasp this truth.

In the social sphere, the object of biopower must be redefined and turned as it were inside out. It will continue to deal with populations rather than with persons. But as institutional power gradually ceases to be national and gravitates to the international plane, the object of biopower will become not the national population seen as the responsibility of the state but *the* population in the most general sense, the totality of the inhabitants of the planet.

Biopower and biopolitics must henceforward focus not on vitality but on mortality, promote not reproduction but reduction, seek not longevity but brevity. The task is historical, philosophical, even metaphysical in scope. The mentality which has dominated the West for two centuries must be transformed; it must become the obverse, the opposite of its former self. It must understand and welcome the necessity of death and seek to prevent life.

We can only describe the needs of the future in terms of our mandate from the Commissioning Parties, giving it the scope and the seriousness it deserves. Whether this vast philosophical movement can come to pass is not for us to say. However, though shifts in mentalities may be notoriously slow, they do change. We have suggested ways of encouraging such a transformation, both individual and societal. This is Conquest in its profoundest sense. He must remain the first of all the Horsemen if the others are to prevail. We now turn to those who ride after him.

II. War

The Second Horseman rides a blood-red steed and wields a great sword; he is the leader of armies. In the Apocalypse, power is given to him 'to take peace from the earth that they should kill one another'. Who is 'they'? Throughout most of history, soldiers fought wars and soldiers got killed. In its modern guise, particularly in our own turbulent century, war annihilates far more civilians than soldiers. In the 1990s alone, at the most conservative estimate, 6 million civilians have been caught in the crossfire of nearly 100 wars.

Along with disease and famine, internecine war is a highly promising Population Reduction Strategy in the modern world as well. The use of external force to 'kill them' should be considered only as a last resort. Today there is no way we can imitate much less equal Genghis Khan, nor should we try even if we could.

Where should the 'kill one another' PRS apply? Certainly not in the North, or only in the most carefully selected areas. Predictably, three-quarters of all investment and most of the world's productive capacity are concentrated in the rich countries. Fomenting war in these wealthy regions would be counterproductive and demand disproportionate political and material resources.

Despite the occasional archaic exception like Bosnia or Kosovo, the prospect of war between or within European countries, or even between Western Europe and Russia, has become nearly as inconceivable as war between the USA and Canada. In contrast, war is not at all outdated in the South or in the new Islamic republics of the former Soviet Union. There it can remain a powerful tool for 'pruning the luxuriant growth'.

Arranging for them to 'kill one another' requires both psychological and physical weapons. We have already touched on the psychological ones, particularly the means of defining the 'self' in 'self-defence'. Identity politics triggers violence; it also diminishes solidarity with the victims of that violence. They become utterly foreign, of a different essence from 'you' and 'me'. Discrimination and oppression targeting particular groups strengthen their sense of self-identity and should, for that reason, be discreetly encouraged. Feeling victimised leads to choosing one's own victims.

Nor should one neglect a relatively recent force we may call 'e-mail', 'remittance' or 'diaspora chauvinists'. Emigré populations frequently possess greater material resources than their former compatriots. They may also harbour guilt feelings at not being in the thick of the nationalist or religious fray 'at home' and compensate by promoting extremist strategies from afar. This phenomenon affects diasporas from American Jews and Palestinians to Canadian Croatians to migrant Tamil Tigers and

European-based Islamic fundamentalists. It is worth encouraging them so long as they confine their activities strictly to their former homelands and do not interfere in the politics of their host countries.

Whatever groups are involved, at home or abroad, one must keep on raising the stakes. It must be made clear that not everyone can get the benefit of such and such a resource, project or investment. In the poor world where most of the recommended strategies will be played out, the continuation of 'development' and 'development projects' as traditionally conceived can be used to good effect.

People displaced by large dams, or deprived through the commercial or ecological erosion of their resource base, become desperate and make excellent recruits for chauvinist, fundamentalist, nationalist or religious leaders. Once they have discovered and forged their separate 'identities', they can be pitted against other groups.

Most of those who were rural dwellers will end up in urban slums. Overpopulation itself, which entails overcrowding, is a further stimulus to strife. For conflict (as well as for hunger and disease to be examined shortly) promising conditions exist in many large Third World cities for developing 'Beirut', 'Algiers' or 'Colombo' models, with ethnic or religious substrata.

Crowding was also instrumental in the rural setting of the Hutu–Tutsi conflict in Rwanda which can be interpreted partly as a resource war. As the then Rwandan agriculture minister said in 1991, long before the tensions had reached the stage of mass killings, 'We have high population pressure and decreasing agricultural productivity due to soil erosion ... we can produce enough food for 5 million people but we have 7.3 million ...' The solution to that arithmetical problem was soon revealed.

Although research shows that fomenting war is complex because no war ever has a single cause, some strong causal patterns can be identified. The Peace Research Institute of Oslo (PRIO) conflict listings show that the 1990s have been rife with armed conflicts (98 from January 1990 to December 1996); these have been overwhelmingly civil wars, not inter-state ones. According to PRIO, conflicts demonstrate the following characteristics:

- They take place chiefly in poor countries where agriculture is still the main contributor to GDP.

- The environmental factors most frequently associated with civil conflict are 'land degradation ... low freshwater availability per capita and high population density', in that order.

- The most war-prone political regimes are, statistically, 'semi-democratic governments'.

- A 'particularly strong correlation exists between high external debt and the incidence of civil war'.

- 'Falling export income from primary commodities is closely associated with the *outbreak* of civil war' (PRIO's emphasis).

- A history of vigorous IMF intervention is also positively linked with all forms of political and armed conflict. 'The number of IMF arrangements and a high conditionality are crucial for the occurrence of both political protest and civil conflict.'[4]

These synergistic, causative factors are made to measure for our purposes. Debt continues to mount. Commodity prices continue to fall, since the exportable products of many competing countries all fall within the same narrow range and create gluts on world markets. The purchasing power of exports is in free fall; Africa can buy only two-thirds as much with export revenues as it could buy in 1980. Petroleum exporters, often thought of as especially well off, can buy only 40 per cent as much on foreign markets as in 1980. The oil exporters are an especially interesting target as most of them cannot diversify their export products. We recommend allowing petroleum prices to fall even lower than they are today.

Rising debts and falling prices lead to partial or total defaults which in turn cause IMF conditionality to become more severe. If previous causative factors hold true, conflicts should also escalate. As we conclude this Report, South-East Asia is being firmly placed in the grip of the IMF, proving that even former 'tigers' are not immune. Their staggering debts and dense populations make them good candidates for major PRS as well.

Indonesia, for example, has the world's fourth largest population and tried to cope with unmanageable numbers for decades through the 'Transmigrasi' programme, sending settlers to outlying islands. It must now hew to the IMF line and will not be able to afford such programmes nor the broad scale corruption which greased so many palms and wheels. This is the same country where in 1965 the army butchered some half a million people in 'anti-communist' pogroms, an interesting precedent.

Elsewhere in poor and populous countries, the high-debt, high-conditionality syndrome has long been present, exacerbating class hatreds and ethnic divisions. Since these countries contribute little or nothing to global welfare, they are precisely those where one seeks to 'prune the luxuriant growth'.

The institutions which design adjustment programmes often pay lip service to the ideals of democratic governance but democracy is largely incompatible with the conditions they insist on. PRIO points guardedly to 'semi-democratic' regimes as characteristic of conflict situations. Governments of poor countries must accept deregulation of their markets and open up to global competition while simultaneously trying to keep their dissatisfied populations under control. Since living standards for the majority are constantly deteriorating, these governments are at risk of violent (not to mention electoral) overthrow. They are thus caught in the triple-bind of 'be democratic', 'apply strict conditionality' and 'stay in power'. This paradox may account for the strong correlation observed by PRIO between 'semi-democratic' political regimes and civil war.

For our purposes, governments must either be convinced or be forced to advance the aims of population control, including summary disposal of their own criminal and anti-social elements and the administration of incentives for sterilisation and contraception (to be discussed later). So long as these functions are properly executed by local authorities, there is no need or justification for direct foreign interference.

Can the curative strategy of war be applied without political hindrance? Will not meddling Northern governments or 'humanitarians' attempt to block it? Such interference may remain a factor in isolated instances, but on the whole, conflicts engendered by ethnic, sub-national or even ecologically-based hatreds and rivalries no longer evoke much sympathy in the North.

The era of strong political opposition and broad solidarity fronts, such as the movements against the Vietnam War or in defence of Chile, Nicaragua or South Africa, is over. In presenting the contemporary battles of the poor, with their confusing politics and apparently random butchery, one should always imply that they occur amongst 'barbarians' and 'savages'. The 'civilised world' should look upon these conflicts as pitiful, childish and insoluble. The West is thus made more cohesive, an additional advantage.

The response of the 'civilised world' to intra-Southern conflicts should nonetheless centre on humanitarian missions. Should this recommendation seem at cross-purposes with our overarching goal, it must be recalled that saving 50 people, preferably on camera, can be a convenient curtain behind which 50,000 may be eliminated. These missions reinforce not only the image of the victims as hopeless weaklings unable to sort out their own affairs but also that of their countries as proper targets (one cannot imagine the USA or Germany as the scene of a humanitarian mission by outsiders ...

Perhaps, in future, humanitarian organisations may also be persuaded to cooperate with birth control programmes, sterilisations and abortions for 'the good of the victims'. The significant trend is the replacement of the 'ethics of solidarity' by the 'ethics of emergency'. Post-colonial pity for the downtrodden and mercy for the afflicted *à la* Mother Teresa have all but supplanted politics of any stripe. The 'afflicted' symbolically occupy the same existential plane as children and mental degenerates. Yet no one can oppose humanitarian aid without appearing utterly heartless. We recommend it be consolidated.

Arms Trade

Whenever and wherever possible, objects of PRS should self-select and deal with one another. This assumes that they will have the physical resources to do so. The Hutus may have got by mostly with machetes, but hand-to-hand elimination is inefficient and sloppy. More sophisticated *matériel* should be made generally available.

A superficial reading of the figures shows that the value of arms transfers to the Third World has plummeted since 1989, with official statistics registering a drop of over 40 per cent in constant dollar terms in the 1990s. These numbers are deceptive. The decline in dollar value does not mean that conflict in these Southern countries has been or will be significantly diminished, quite the contrary. Since the end of the Cold War, Third World arms purchases from official or unofficial sources reflect:

- The need for many beleaguered Southern governments to improve their internal security and counter-insurgency capacities. They have switched from heavy external combat equipment like tanks and planes to less expensive infantry weapons, helicopters and riot control gear for use against their own increasingly restive people.

- The new productive capacity of smaller, cheaper, non-traditional arms suppliers who have benefited from technology transfers in the past. Many belligerents, even if they fall under official embargos, can now satisfy most of their military needs much closer to home.

- A spectacular rise of the arms black market and an equally dramatic drop in prices, so that an AK-47 which might have cost $100 can now be picked up for $30–40 in Russia or even $8–10 on the Cambodian black market. Black markets used to be far more expensive than legal ones but this is no longer the case. Arms purchasers need not pay costly premiums to escape detection.

During the Cold War, most weapons systems were massive, expensive and bought to be stockpiled. In sharp contrast to the Pentagon and the Soviet military of the old days, today's arms purchasers are buying smaller, less sophisticated items for immediate use. The United States remains the pre-eminent official supplier for both large and small war *matériel* and has been the big winner of the commercial Cold War. For relatively small quantities, the US retail arms market remains the top favourite as well since it harbours hundreds of legal arms manufacturers, importers and 285,000 licensed dealers. Over 500 million small arms of all types are in circulation worldwide, more than half of them in the USA. Russia has lost out completely in this market. In the past decade, its official orders from the Third World have plunged by over 80 per cent.

To achieve economies of scale, many weapons firms in other countries are merging, buying out competitors or setting up joint ventures and strategic alliances for transferring military technology. Major beneficiaries include the Balkans, the Indian subcontinent and Central Asia in addition to the already well-armed Middle East.

Despite the tendency to reduce armouries, many Third World nations are acquiring not just small arms but weapons of mass destruction. The US intelligence community now suspects at least ten countries of possessing biological weapons in spite of the theoretical ban imposed by the Biological and Toxin Weapons Convention. Any country which possesses the skills of trained biotechnologists, commercial fermentation facilities and a pharmaceuticals industry, or even enough competence to run a foreign-supplied drugs factory, is perfectly capable of producing biological weapons. Such weapons need not even be stockpiled. They can be quickly and cheaply produced on demand in small factories. Delivery systems can range from the sophisticated to the crude (particularly in the case of terrorists prepared to sacrifice themselves).

In the unofficial small conventional arms markets, a growing professional caste is made up of virtuoso traffickers, expert in concealing consignments, designing complex shipping routes, counterfeiting documents and laundering money. For larger quantities of off-the-books purchases, major market centres include Bangkok, Peshawar, Turkey and several ex-Soviet Republics.

Authorities in the developed and underdeveloped countries alike appear both unwilling and unable to curb any aspect of the lucrative arms trade. Not surprisingly, the United Nations has got no further than establishing a harmless voluntary 'register' of conventional arms transfers. We foresee no major obstacles to weapons procurement by governments, dissident groups or criminal gangs anywhere wishing to take military matters into their own hands. Although the arms trade may have shifted some of its bases, we agree with the expert who declares that it 'will continue to flourish in the years ahead, with few barriers to its continued development and growth'.

This being so, one should let nature take its course, while giving arms supplies a discrete push and occasional pump-priming financial assistance here and there. Low- and high-tech weapons are spreading among the less developed countries, a desirable development so long as they turn them on each other.[5]

Intervention

Despite their demonstrated propensity to 'kill one another', the 'barbarians' will not oblige us entirely in this regard and certainly not to the requisite degree. Furthermore, they can still do us great harm. They will often be full of hatred for Western civilisation, better organised than they used to be and equipped with the rich proceeds of their multifarious criminal activities.

From time to time, Western powers will be obliged to intervene in their affairs and the Western public should grow used to this idea. While we may still have to fight the occasional Iraq, our chief opponents will, in the words of one analyst, be 'groups whom we today call terrorists, guerillas, bandits and robbers, but who will undoubtedly hit upon more formal titles to describe themselves'.[6]

Some future wars will take place between traditional states and these new barbarians; the warlords, druglords and organised gangs of all kinds who are henceforward *in competition with the nation-state*. In some cases, although traditional authorities refuse to recognise the fact, they have *already* replaced the state, or have so permeated it that the two are virtually indistinguishable. ('More and more governments are being overwhelmed by, run by, or supplanted by an astonishing variety of criminal organisations and innovative structures for controlling wealth through violence and coercion.')

These organisations are fast, mobile and ignore frontiers. ('The borders we see on maps increasingly do not exist on the ground.') The West's new targets will be continent-spanning Mafias, whether Russian-Ukrainian, Albanian or Kosovar, Nigerian or Italian; Japanese Yakuza or Chinese Triads; Colombian or Mexican drug cartels or simply the estimated 1.5 million US gang members.

The growing power of these post-state organisations will challenge the conventional state through various transnational mercenary links. They will increasingly defend regional, even worldwide ambitions. Fewer classic wars will occur but greater violence and genuine strategic threats will be commonplace.

These threats should be publicised rather than hidden or dismissed as they too often are today. Western governments err when they pretend to have the situation well in hand. Instead of glossing over the dangers, they should prepare their people for undertaking necessary interventions and to that end should make the citizenry feel threatened.

Shaping public opinion should be relatively simple because the threat is genuine. The new barbarians are increasingly sophisticated and will not hesitate to use whatever weapons of mass destruction they may have at their disposal. If the World Trade Center bombers had packed their van with radioactive material, the New York financial district would have had to be sealed off for decades. If they had chosen toxic or biological agents, no one can say what hecatomb might have resulted.

We in the West are woefully unprepared to take on these post-state organisations and criminal armies. Having spent decades developing technologies to put huge distances between ourselves and our potential enemies, (long-range bombers, missiles, and so on), we should wake up to the fact that the military targets of twenty-first-century combat will be close up. Warfare will be more like *The Iliad* than Hiroshima.

We do not need new bombers, submarines or tanks, unless it is to keep defence industry workers in jobs. We do need to redirect funds towards real defence of our interests and towards the strategies outlined here. Tragically, we are far better at killing a few hundred people at a great remove than at targeting our real enemies at close range. ('Our current system amounts to punishing the murderer's neighbourhood while letting the murderer go free.') Let us add that the attack against the 'murderer' should ideally appear to come from one of his near neighbours so as to provoke resentment and retaliation against other barbarians.

Post-modern warfare is likely to take place far less in deserts or other wide open spaces than in urban environments where the enemy knows the terrain and its inhabitants far better than we do. That terrain will include high-rise slums, tunnels, subways and sewers; it will be vertical whereas conventional warfare has been almost exclusively horizontal. It will also be filthy and disease-ridden. ('The likeliest battlefields are cityscapes where human waste goes undisposed, the air is appalling and mankind is rotting.')

Americans, in particular, have got used to having machines, not men, do the dirty work. They now expect zero casualties from warfare; whereas in future, the soldier will again become all-important. The urban battlefield cannot be fought for, taken or held without soldiers getting killed.

Even the ethical mindset of the West is ill adapted to fighting foreseeable future foes. Our courts unhesitatingly afford legal, constitutional protection to foreign druglords and other criminals. We follow laws and rules of engagement; they do not. ('Increasingly, the world doesn't give a damn about our laws, customs or table manners ... We are constrained by a past century's model of what armies do, what police do, and what governments legally can do. Our opponents have none of this baggage.')

The battlefields of the future will not all be in foreign theatres. We are likely to confront the same problems and the same unpreparedness at home. ('An archipelago of failure is emerging within the United States, posing problems so intractable and concentrated that traditional law enforcement may prove unable to contain them.') Cities in other Western nations are far from immune to this blight and witness helplessly the spread of their own archipelagos of failure.[7]

Wealthy Americans have already sensed the danger. Well ahead of the game, they have moved into 30,000 gated, guarded communities. A further 60,000 such enclaves are on the drawing boards for construction before the year 2005. Yet even behind their walls, neither the privileged of the USA nor other Westerners will escape the snares of twenty-first-century conflict.

We will not speculate on the links that the Commissioning Parties may have forged with Western military or law enforcement leadership. We nonetheless feel bound to counsel certain strategies consonant with our overall mandate. No part of this Report is political or science fiction. We are, rather, addressing the threat and the enemy we confront *today*.

The familiar, nineteenth-century world of stable nations with no lawless, extra-state, trans-state and post-state competitors is disappearing, probably for good. Our militaries must stop preparing for war with the USSR or the Gulf War and take the twenty-first century seriously. We must also rethink the respective roles of the police and the army.

Earlier, we highlighted the need for a strong international executive to replace an outworn United Nations. The 'peacekeeping' model of the UN has repeatedly proved ineffectual; it is time to develop a new concept. Like any executive, the proposed new international one should command a sizeable, well-trained and well-equipped armed intervention force prepared for the kind of combat missions we have described. Such a force would have strong selling points: not only could it fight international crime and terrorism, thus making the world safer for everyone (except for the sponsors of criminal activity), but it would also indirectly protect the nation-state. For governments not yet bought or replaced by Mafias, this should be a convincing argument.

We also urge Western governments to consider the establishment and use of *private security offensive and defensive forces* in parallel to their regular uniformed troops. Embryonic structures of this kind already exist, such as, for example, the South Africa-based firm called 'Executive Outcomes'. Such forces were historically common; they were called mercenaries. We are not speaking merely of security guards or 'rent-a-cop' companies but of actual combat troops. They should serve state objectives and not be biddable by private entities. Governments singly or jointly would be their only clients. Public recourse to private companies for such forces would have numerous advantages:

- They would provide outlets for unemployed, disaffected, frequently violent youth, discipline them and give them something socially constructive to do.

- They would have to bid competitively for contracts. For a great many non-traditional missions they would cost far less than our present bloated and over-equipped militaries.

- They would not be burdened with hampering laws and established rules of engagement but could get the job done quickly, cleanly and efficiently.

- Because their employees knew the risks when they took their well-paid jobs, casualties would not attract undue attention or public outcry as does the death of the lowliest recruit today.

Armed combat troops (as opposed to a peacekeeping force) at the service of an international executive and recourse to private fighting firms by governments may seem a long way off, but these proposals are not far-fetched and we believe that their advantages will be rapidly perceived. The US State Department, for example, has already signed a multi-million dollar contract with the US company 'Military Professional Resources, Inc.' for the training of Bosnian Muslim–Croat Federation military forces. This line of action should be vigorously pursued until it comes to seem normal or at least one of a range of standard operating procedures.

Realistically speaking and for some time to come, however, the bulk of military engagements will be undertaken by traditional state armies whose responsibility will be to defend Western society and culture against all hostile comers. The lucid officer cited above recognises that 'The *de facto* role of the US armed forces will be to keep the world safe for our economy and open to our cultural assault. To those ends, we will do a fair amount of killing.'[8]

Barbarian Babies?

If killing must be done, what comes afterwards? Will not the 'barbarians' simply make up for lost time once the conflict has subsided? Will they not then produce offspring fast and furiously? We should briefly address the so-called 'post-conflict birth syndrome' which has historically caused birth rates to soar in recently devastated societies. If China's population could recover after Ghengis Khan, what might be the ultimate impact of contemporary PRS?

The reactive baby boom appears to be a notion left over from ancient and medieval history or from the Second World War, with scant relevance to the present. According to UN data, there is little post-conflict change in crude birth rates – except in a downward direction – in war-torn countries as diverse as

Vietnam, Nicaragua, Iran, Iraq, Mozambique, South Africa or even (after a brief spurt) in extreme cases of post-genocidal societies like East Timor and Cambodia. The exception is Palestine where a politically dictated natalist policy is clearly being followed by the population. Elsewhere, it appears that for our purposes, conflict and the arms trade will have an exclusively positive impact.

We turn now to another Population Reduction Strategy which has been both a cause and a consequence of warfare: the hunger and famine factor.

III. Famine

The Third Horseman mounts a black horse, carries a pair of scales and a voice cries out, 'A denier for a measure of wheat, a denier for three measures of barley.' Saint John's vision of famine is surprisingly contemporary: both in the Bible and in today's world, who eats and who starves is determined not by the vagaries of weather, blight or even war but by politics and purchasing power. When the voice cries out 'A denier for a measure of wheat', it knows what the traffic will bear. For those who have the power to command it and the deniers to pay for it, food is always readily available.

Throughout most of history, in all societies, food crises were common. In medieval Europe, a measure of seed might yield only two measures of grain, harvests were meagre, reserves easily exhausted and famines occurred roughly every ten or twelve years. Still, on the whole, 'no one starved unless everyone did'.

Modern famine responds far more to market forces than to absolute physical scarcities and rarely strikes the well-off. During the great Irish potato famine of 1846–47 which killed close to 1 million people, large landowners routinely exported food to Britain as poor peasants dropped all around them.

Even in 'classic' twentieth-century Third World famines like that of Bengal in 1943 which killed several millions, wealthy tables remained laden. During the African famines of the 1980s, one never heard of massive deaths among bureaucrats, businessmen and army officers ... In the North or South today it would take a rare combination of circumstances – utterly failed harvests plus a shutdown of trade due to war or similar calamity – to reduce the rich to malnourishment, much less starvation.

Our concern here is to test the value of the traditional scourge of famine as a population curb. Malthus saw the failure of food production to keep pace with human reproduction as the *only* reliable 'check' on runaway births. For our part, we believe that the 'green weapon' can be targeted more accurately than ever before but it is not the only one at our disposal. It should not be conceived in isolation but as part of an arsenal.

Depending on whether food is scarce or plentiful, the conflicts analysed above (and the diseases to be examined below) will be fuelled or dampened, exacerbated or attenuated. The Horsemen ride together, helping each other to trample their victims.

Intellectual confusion and unrealistic sentimentality cloud far too many discussions of hunger and famine and pervade the more recent, utopian notion of 'food security'.[9] To begin by asking – as so many pundits do – if in future 'the world' can produce enough food for 8, 10 or 12 billion people is well-nigh meaningless. For a price, with sufficient political power brought to bear, 'the world' can do virtually anything.

The relevant questions concern not just physical resources such as land, water, agricultural inputs, seeds and the like, however important these may be, but also political and financial access to food and to land to grow it on, for countries, social classes and individuals. We shall deal with these aspects using the traditional economic categories of supply and demand.

Supply

In a few recent, outstanding years, world harvests have reached a record-setting 1,900 million tonnes of food grains. If roots and tubers are added, production of basic crops (wheat, maize, rice, millet, sorghum, potatoes, cassava) may be as high as 2,500 million tonnes, a noteworthy improvement (of almost 40 per cent) compared to 1980. The steadily upward production trend of past decades seems, however, set to be reversed, to the point that we foresee chronic food shortages in the new millennium.

Despite the embarrassment suffered by previous study groups which prophesied penury and were proven wrong, we take the risk again because a host of factors points in that direction. After years of running neck and neck, the old Malthusian truth has come back into play: population growth rates now outstrip increases in food production.

Grain carryover stocks are relatively precarious. The FAO recommends they be kept stable at 20 per cent, or 73 days of world consumption. In 1995–96, after three years of declining harvests, a red flare went up. Global stocks dropped to 48 days of consumption, their lowest level in 20 years; wheat and maize prices soared. Harvests and stocks rebounded in the 1996–97 season and prices returned to 'normal'. We predict that this will be a temporary spurt, not a lasting improvement.

Production is more likely to stabilise or decline while populations continue to grow. By definition, no country has unlimited supplies of land, water, energy, fertilisers and farmers. Now even some of the best endowed are finding their natural limits stretched.

Limits to Land

The world's foremost cereals producers are, in descending order, China, the United States, India, Russia, Indonesia, France, Canada, Brazil, Germany, Ukraine, Australia. Save perhaps in Brazil and the USA, they have little room for expansion of overall farming area. On the contrary, much excellent cropland is being steadily eroded, polluted, salinised or paved over. If further production increases are to occur they will mostly have to be squeezed out of the land that is left.

China has made tremendous strides over the past 15 years, boosting its food production by almost 50 per cent. In 1980, China's production was equal to that of the USA; today Chinese grow half again as much food as Americans. Nearly three-quarters of the economically active population is required to accomplish this feat whereas fewer than 3 per cent of Americans are farmers.

Now China is bent on industrialising at breakneck speed. Although it can, like the United States, substitute man-made for human capital, we strongly doubt that it can repeat its food production performance of the recent past and may not even be able to sustain it. As for other producers, the USA grows little more grain today than in 1980 (partly, it is true, due to subsidies for fallowed land). The American, Canadian and Australian breadbaskets are all rain-fed and climate-sensitive, a precarious position in times of global warming.

Russia and the Ukraine are also weather-dependent and their production plunged as soon as Soviet state-farm subsidies were withdrawn. Intensive cereal cropping in Europe also relies heavily on subsidies, still the most onerous item in the Community budget. Ecological disasters in Indonesia and Green Revolution[10] fatigue in India will further depress progress.

In past decades, a good part of improved global grain output was due to high-yielding, high-input Green Revolution plant varieties. Some experts point out that there is still plenty of scope for these varieties (or genetically modified seeds) to be grown where they have never been tried, for example in Africa. In a few virgin territories like the Brazilian cerrado, new acid-tolerant, drought-resistant seeds might one day make Brazil self-sufficient in wheat and perhaps an exporter as well.

The same experts also claim that new land can be put to the plough elsewhere, that irrigation and double or triple cropping in poorer countries will boost yields. They trust in technology and see no cause for alarm, often failing to note that deforestation and over-grazing expose land to erosion, while 'double-cropping' often turns out to be 'over-cropping'. All these contribute to declining fertility.

Such optimistic predictions overlook several other crucial factors. Although the USA and Brazil may be able to expand crop areas, the law of diminishing returns applies there as elsewhere. Each extra unit of output will cost more to produce than the previous one. The little land remaining to be farmed in poorer countries is of relatively poorer quality and often located far from markets in areas lacking basic infrastructure. 'Dirt farmers' might be willing to settle such lands for want of anything better, but without costly investments in infrastructure and inputs, large-scale commercial farming seems a poor bet.

Limits to Water

We are also told that irrigation can make up for losses elsewhere and raise production as it has done in the past. A mere 16 per cent of farmland is irrigated worldwide (two and a half times more than in 1950) but supplies fully one-third of total food crops. However, fresh water is in increasingly short supply, and competition, not to say open warfare to secure it, is heating up between nations as well as between agricultural, industrial and individual users. Technical agriculture experts tend to ignore sociological and political constraints.

Physically speaking, fresh water is poorly distributed between countries and continents. Irrigation presently hogs nearly three-quarters of all the fresh water. In the South, agriculture accounts for 90 per cent of water use. How long can this lopsided resource-capture pattern prevail as Third World people flock to cities?

In the Chinese countryside, in spite of its disproportionally favoured position, tens of millions of peasants in the Northern provinces already suffer chronic water shortages. Present or potential scarcity of water for agriculture is hardly confined to China, although the Chinese have been forced to remove at least a million hectares of irrigated land from production. Other countries, from Mexico to Algeria, are similarly affected. Waste and poor management contribute markedly to scarcity but absolute physical constraints bind ever more tightly.

Aquifers are drying up. Fossil water under the US Great Plains is already half depleted. Once fertile land in Texas, Israel and India has been abandoned for want of ground water. In the former USSR, where the Aral Sea was drained in order to irrigate cotton, close to 3 million hectares have turned to salt desert and can no longer be farmed.

Governments will have trouble justifying profligate irrigation schemes when hundreds of millions of urban people lack drinking water. Most irrigation is both inefficient and costly, with crops actually absorbing little more than one-third of the water applied. Even when irrigation systems still have plentiful water to draw on, maintenance is expensive and requires constant attention to silted-up channels and dams.

From the Aral Sea fiasco to many of India's previously high-yielding Green Revolution areas, salt build-up is common and destroys fertility. In the Sahel, at the behest of the World Bank, land once carefully tended under communal ownership has been privatised at bargain prices. Cheap land, the proximity of rivers and easy credit for irrigated rice-growing have attracted get-rich-quick merchants using makeshift, no-drainage irrigation systems that can ruin tens of thousands of hectares in a season or two. In short, the Green Revolution appears to be turning brown and global warming may well wither it further.

As for other key inputs, fertiliser and pesticide run-offs are already poisoning drinking water supplies in many regions in the North, further sharpening conflict between farm and non-farm water users.

Limits to Money

Powerful economic and social forces also constrain supply. Land ownership, like ownership of other assets, is highly concentrated in the hands of wealthier landlords and has grown more so in the past generation as the Green Revolution has enriched the already rich. Poor people lack access to land and could not intensify cultivation even if they were willing to work harder.

Improved seeds and requisite technologies for improving food output will hardly be given away. As with the initial Green Revolution, new agricultural practices will be costly and available only to better-off farmers. These techniques must be spread through complex institutional networks which are difficult to build and sustain in times of national austerity. Even if production *per se* improves, more expensive technologies necessarily produce more expensive food.

Countries with heavy debt burdens do not have the funds to invest in costly development of new land nor can they subsidise the kinds of agricultural extension and improved technology programmes which could help traditional farmers to produce more. Agricultural research and development were responsible for the major part of improved yields in the post-war world, but research and development funding, which was increasing by 7 per cent a year in the 1970s has stagnated in the 1990s.

For all these reasons, we foresee severe, multiple and self-reinforcing constraints on supply accompanied by escalating conflicts over land and water. The optimists may be correct that in the aggregate, world food supply can keep pace with world food demand *expressed in money*. But money is precisely what the poor do not have. They have needs, they may be hungry, but the market is deaf to that kind of 'demand'. We now turn to this aspect of the world food equation.

Demand

Can 'the world' feed its present population of 6 billion with present harvests? This question too is pointless because it all depends on what is meant by 'feed'. If it means that production is divided so that everyone is allocated an identical vegetarian ration of grain or tubers, with minimum protein supplied by peas, beans and pulses for a barely adequate total of 2,350 calories a day, then the answer is yes. Under circumstances of absolute equality and universal willingness to consume a basic, monotonous, barely life-sustaining diet, 'the world' can feed its present population and then some.[11]

If it means instead that one-quarter of everyone's diet comes from animal products (which are 'concentrated calories') and that people are also able to consume a variety of fruit, vegetables and oils (and from our privileged position we would add wines and beers), then the answer is definitely no. In that case, assuming present harvests, 'the world' can only feed a shade over 3 billion people, approximately half as many as are currently alive. Whatever the scenario, it is purely academic to proceed as if food supplies were ever going to be equally apportioned and as if those who can afford a more satisfying regime would be content with nothing but meagre portions of staple grains and legumes.

We are not concerned here with biological need, or only in so far as its denial can contribute to higher mortality. Food demand must be examined strictly in the light of purchasing power since food is a commodity like any other. Those who can afford to eat as they please are rarely vegetarians. Statistically speaking, they never are. In all societies, at all times, when extra income becomes available, it is spent on improved diets. As the better-off express their demand, in hard cash, for more animal products, the supply side follows that demand.

Arable land is then converted to pasture. Despite the presence of large numbers of hungry or malnourished people in many countries, affluent command over food means that animal feed crops displace basic food crops: sorghum for cattle replaces maize for people in Mexico, soya replaces black beans in Brazil, cassava is planted instead of rice in Thailand, and so on.

These crops are frequently exported as feedstuffs for Northern livestock. Changes in land use directly mirror conflicts over food between richer and poorer consumers, wherever they may live. The poor lose doubly: not only can they not afford animal products but the price of their own staple foods rises as their production area decreases.

Moralists proceed as if everyone 'ought' to eat the same basic, boring diet so as somehow to accommodate the poor. Virtuous, self-appointed spokespersons enjoy pointing accusing fingers at Western pets which are better fed than many human beings. So they are, since their masters are free to spend their incomes as they see fit.

The dogs-and-cats argument is a variation on the theme of denouncing 'luxury' food exports from poor, 'hungry' countries to supply affluent tables in the North. Not surprisingly, it has never been shown how fewer dogs and cats or fewer strawberries and avocados in December could place a single square meal in the belly of a single destitute person who lacked the means to pay for it.

Food Trade and Aid

As for aggregate demand from solvent sources, commercial grain imports have remained remarkably stable for over a decade at about 200 million tonnes a year. For countries experiencing shortfalls and financially unable to purchase enough grain on commercial markets, food aid in the 1990s has been relatively generous (between 10 and 15 million tonnes a year).

We believe these factors are set to change. Commercial imports by solvent, food-deficit countries will increase, whereas food aid always decreases as supplies grow tighter. The food aid record was set in the plentiful year 1993 when 16.8 million tonnes were given away or sold on concessional terms worldwide.

By 1996–97, however, smaller harvests had caused food aid to plunge to 7.5 million tonnes, down one-quarter from the previous year and a sign of things to come. According to the US Department of Agriculture, 65 countries containing roughly half the world's population already need 22 million tonnes of food aid if their basic nutritional needs are considered.

China is once more a crucial factor in the equation. Ominously, although it is the world's largest grain producer, China is now second only to Japan for cereal imports. Korea, Egypt, Brazil and Mexico follow these top two Asian customers:

all now have serious financial problems. Lester Brown, one of the best known latter-day Malthusians, makes a strong and plausible case to show that China will become the single largest destabilising actor on the world food scene.

Some of Brown's images are striking: if China is to attain its official goal of increasing annual egg consumption from 100 to 200 per person per year, it will take a flock of 1.3 billion hens gobbling the equivalent of the entire grain output of Australia (about 26 million tonnes). If every adult Chinese quaffs just three more beers a year, the bar bill will be an extra million tonnes of grain.[12]

The impact of Chinese dietary improvement will thus be monumental for the rest of the world. Since China officially switched its agricultural policy in 1978 'from a system of collective responsibility to one of family responsibility', China's progress has been spectacular. The law of higher animal products consumption inexorably following increasing wealth applies to China in spades. Between 1978 and 1992, per capita pork consumption was multiplied by nearly two and a half, despite a population increase of 200 million. Other upmarket food items have registered similar growth in demand.

China has also decided, disastrously in our view, to develop a car-centred transport system. Millions of farmland hectares are destined to be converted to highways and car parks. In the rapidly industrialising south, huge, fertile acreage which regularly produced two or three crops a year is already being lost to urbanisation and pollution, probably to the tune of a million hectares a year.

China is therefore unlikely to remain self-sufficient in food. But it is eminently solvent and can afford, at current prices, to import whatever amounts of grain it may require. Lester Brown provides another startling comparison: China's trade surplus with the United States alone – $30 billion in 1994 – would have allowed it to buy *all the grain on world markets that year*. China's cash reserves and potential import needs are precisely the problem for other needy clients.

Chinese demand for grain is expected to increase by one-third between now and 2020, from 450 to 594 million tonnes. Because of dietary improvements 40 per cent of that demand will be for feed grains. An importer of just 3 million tonnes of cereals in 1991, China's purchases are expected to shoot up to 40 million tonnes by 2000 before stabilising at about 43 million in 2010, or so say experts (two Chinese and one American) reporting to the OECD.

Depending on many variables, including weather, introduction of high-yielding varieties, more or less efficient feed-to-meat conversion, rates of urbanisation, speed of dietary change and population growth, these projections could be too low or too high. They still indicate the trend. National defence and ideology also demand that the Chinese government keep a close eye on the balance between self-sufficiency and imports.[13]

Here, then, is a huge and powerful country undergoing rapid industrial development, with an already substantial middle class. Will it seek to satisfy its own consumers despite the financial or human costs for other people beyond its borders? China will have a redoubtable capacity to affect world grain stocks and prices.

If, as we foresee, China's demand does force up prices in the medium term, the increase could prove burdensome, even catastrophic, for a number of the West's major allies. Japan's food import needs have stabilised but they are not going to diminish. Major buyers like Korea and Mexico are now members of the OECD; both are victims of financial crisis and the West cannot afford to let them down. Egypt, another large importer, is the key to Middle East stability. With the possible exception of Korea, whose purchasing power has been sharply curtailed by devaluation, the commercial demand of all these food importers is expected to mount as their populations grow.

Like any other production, grain production naturally responds to market signals. Yet even with more remunerative prices, there are no guarantees that world supply could rise to meet vastly increased demand. A further, little noticed destabilising factor is rural-to-urban outmigration. You can make a worker out of a peasant; you cannot make a peasant out of a worker. Except in parts of Africa, once a peasant has become a city-dweller he does not return to the countryside and, if he tries, he finds that his place has been taken.

One can also substitute capital for labour. This is why fewer than 3 per cent of Americans still farm. But countries must first have in hand the cash to invest in machinery and fertiliser.

We foresee rising demand and hogging of supply by solvent customers, resulting in higher prices and creating fresh tensions between have and have-not nations, between Ins and Outs in individual societies.

Solutions and Recommendations

These trends of supply and demand are almost entirely favourable to our purposes. Where is extra PRS effort required?

Erosion, salinisation, pollution and urbanisation will continue under their own steam. Sustaining and stimulating them will require little more than *status quo* policies and financial drain (including debt and debt service) so that they contribute to limiting food supply and raising prices.

Market monopolisation by a few solvent buyers like China and Japan will also serve the objectives of scarcity and higher food prices. Given the free market and the capacity of these paying customers to cover their food needs financially, we cannot say exactly where the victims of hunger might be concentrated except that they would match our chief target group of superfluous people in poor countries.

Despite the factors holding back food output, certain policies could significantly bolster it. We recommend that the Commissioning Parties concentrate on blocking these avenues.

Prevention of Cures

Despite limitations of land, water and capital, a hidden food resource exists with genuine potential for low-cost improvement of agricultural supply. Post-harvest losses of grains and other foods now range from 8 to 25 per cent of total crops harvested, depending on the country and the climate. Huge tonnages are spoiled because of poor storage techniques unable to cope with onslaughts of fungi, insects, rodents and other pests.

The more centralised the storage, the greater the opportunities for loss. Development projects and transfers of agricultural technology to dependent countries should seek to downgrade local village and on-farm storage in favour of large, centralised, urban-based facilities where infestations can spread faster and do more damage. Reduced buffer stocks also contribute to higher prices and diminish access to food. Drastic reduction of post-harvest losses would be highly cost-effective and should be prevented.

The second approach which could enhance food access for significant numbers of people is political, that is, land reform and support for small farmers, particularly female farmers. This counter-strategy is less threatening to PRS than it would have been a few decades ago, now that most governments have opted for sweeping Green Revolution-type schemes favouring politically influential commercial farmers and better endowed areas. Donors for their own reasons have also pushed these policies so that small farmers are now at a greater disadvantage than ever.

Whereas land reform was a live issue in many countries two or three decades ago, we see little danger of its revival today. Not only are there now fewer peasants but the peasantry's political capacity to resist market forces has significantly diminished. Governments have learned to respect stringent structural adjustment rules and they now subject agriculture to the same liberal policies as any other sector.

For example, in Egypt, a recently adopted law largely abrogates land reform measures of previous decades so that rents are once more market-determined and landowners can expel at will tenants who once enjoyed unlimited, even hereditary tenure.

Mexican land reform was enshrined in the sacrosanct Article 27 of the Constitution which created *ejidos* or communal village lands with individual use rights. Now Article 27 has been 'reformed' as part of the policies designed to support the North American Free Trade Agreement (NAFTA). The adapted Constitution allows privatisation and foreign ownership of *ejido* land and has opened cooperatives and communal land to the same market forces as any other real estate. The effects are beginning to take hold: in 1995, staple maize production had stagnated and Mexico imported a record 10 million tonnes of grain, more than one-quarter of its annual consumption.

Some opposition movements like the much romanticised Chiapas rebellion in Mexico refuse to accept these facts of life. We tend to see such protests as a last gasp rather than a second wind. Farmers must compete in the marketplace like everyone else. The legal instruments to facilitate this competition are virtually all in place; most governments are under pressure to liberalise food trade and open their markets to (momentarily) cheap imports. In any event, these governments prefer to see their farmers producing valuable export crops rather than the raw material for tortillas.

So long as these conditions hold, land concentration and smallholder invisibility should remain the order of the day. Since these 'invisible farmers' are the only actors who, given technical and political support, could significantly increase yields and local food availability, this is all to the good.

Ideologically speaking, if it is discussed at all, land reform should be presented as yesterday's issue, now superseded by agribusiness efficiency. Peasant farming and its techniques should be dismissed as backward and obsolete. But which techniques, exactly, are modern? This question leads us to the major and much misunderstood area of biotechnology and genetically manipulated crops with regard to which we espouse a possibly unwelcome point of view.

Pandora's Box

Many observers and numerous transnational chemical, pharmaceutical and seed corporations are touting the use of biotechnology and genetic engineering as the latest panacea for combating world hunger. We wish to state our wholehearted support for biologically engineered crops *so long as these plants are grown exclusively in the South where the aim is to reduce food availability and to increase hunger and famine as a population check*. So far, exactly the opposite strategy has been applied: genetically modified crops are rapidly spreading in the North but are considered 'too sophisticated' or 'too expensive' for use in the South.

At the risk of incurring the displeasure of the Commissioning Parties who may have ties to participating industries, we cannot approve the narrow, short-term interests of a part of the transnational business community. We see them acting against the larger interests of the globalised economic system.

Despite space constraints which preclude a full review of the scientific literature concerning biotechnology and genetically modified plants, we shall seek briefly to justify this position. The evidence with which we have been confronted has nonetheless convinced us that plant genetic engineering will backfire, no matter what corporate scientists may claim.

These modified plants can be efficient weapons, yes, but *against those who employ them. In vitro* laboratory experiments and limited field trials cannot reproduce or substitute for the complexities of the environment *in vivo*. We see not merely risks but future 'side-effects' so serious that they will vastly outweigh any benefits that might be gained from the use of these varieties.

Genetically engineered herbicide tolerance in plants (the characteristic which allows whole fields to be sprayed at any time during the growing cycle, theoretically killing weeds but leaving the valuable crop intact) will rapidly breed pest resistance and superweeds. In 1993–94, herbicide tolerance was the plant trait tested for in 36 per cent of field release trials.

A 'weed' (which under different circumstances might be a desirable plant) repeatedly exposed to a given weedkiller will develop tolerance to that product so that higher and higher doses will be required to control it. Constant spraying will leave mounting chemical residues in soil and on crops. Herbicides are known to reduce soil fertility, kill earthworms and beneficial insects, and to pollute water.

Biologically modified plants releasing their own insecticides as opposed to tolerating Brand X herbicide (32 per cent of field trials concerned this trait in 1993–94) are the vegetable equivalent of a constant chemical spray. Such plants can eventually kill a broad range of organisms, including helpful ones. The toxins they emit can survive in soil for long periods and remain potent for several months after the crop itself has been harvested. This means that insects will also be exposed to them throughout their lifespans.

Constant exposure creates strong selection pressures for toxin-resistant 'superbugs' which may then begin to feed on crops other than the one which was originally their exclusive prey. According to its own manufacturer (Monsanto), an engineered insecticide-releasing cotton plant widely sown in the Southern USA kills 80 per cent of cotton bollworms. Yet as one scientist points out, 'eighty per cent mortality is exactly what researchers use when they want to breed resistant insects'.[14]

Scientists once believed that cross-species gene transfers were impossible; they are now known to be common. Because genes do not stay put, resistance effects could spread to a broad variety of organisms – plants, animals and, conceivably, humans. Travelling genes, crossed with superweeds could produce invasive hybrids. Once a gene has escaped into the larger environment it cannot be recalled. Similarly, plants bred to resist specific viruses can lead to the development, through recombination, of new and more virulent viruses than those occurring naturally.

Prior to general release, it was discovered quite by chance that a 'harmless' bacterium (*Klebsiella planticola*), when genetically modified, provoked unexpected changes in soil ecosystems. The bacterium encouraged explosive reproduction of potentially seed-destroying nematodes. Fortunately, in this case, field trials were limited to experimental plots.

One variety of corn has already been bred to resist antibiotics; it is not yet known if this resistance can be conferred on other organisms further up the food chain, including humans. Current knowledge of ecological systems and unintended side-effects is primitive.

In our view, the undesirable consequences of genetically engineered plants is a matter of 'when', not 'if'. Although many of these plants have already 'escaped' and although many corporate scientists will strongly disagree, we urge that use of genetically engineered crops, if they are to be cultivated at all, be confined to poor and populous countries, otherwise these countries will have the last laugh.

Roads Less Travelled

Among other PRS based on food and hunger, we stress the following:

- *Further trade liberalisation.* Agricultural free trade places poorer and weaker Third World farmers in much more direct competition with their highly mechanised counterparts in the North. The latter, in spite of international rules, will probably continue to receive disguised or overt subsidies as well. Within a few years, large quantities of low-priced, imported cereals on local markets should wipe out many borderline, vulnerable smallholders.

- *'Modern' agricultural techniques and reduction of crop variety.* One must counter the small farmer's tendency to save seeds in order to ensure genetic variety, if need be by supplying below cost or free, genetically uniform 'modern' seeds. Pests thrive in circumstances of homogeneity, monocultures are more susceptible to disease than mixed or inter-cropping. Export agriculture is almost always based on uniformity; food crops should be forced to follow the same patterns.

- *Reinforcement of the 'Green Revolution'.* Green Revolution techniques initially increase yields but they require purchased seeds and manufactured inputs which are usually beyond the reach of smaller, poorer cultivators. The latter can also be discouraged through higher rents, cancellation of tenure and other counter-land reform measures.

- *Food aid*, though diminishing, can still be used to good effect if the all-important matter of timing is properly understood. Food aid should arrive just before or coincide with local harvests. Even if these harvests are more meagre than expected, sizeable quantities of foreign food will drive local prices below remunerative levels for local farmers. Charitable agencies can be recruited to assist with distribution. Where imported seeds have come to be relied on, their delivery should also be timed to coincide with inappropriate planting periods.

Famine

Contrary to common belief, full-scale famines are relatively rare. This is why we have concentrated far more on the potential for limiting food supplies and provoking hunger and malnutrition which, if they do not kill outright, provide the favourable terrain for the fourth ancient Horseman, Pestilence, whose modern counterpart we shall encounter in the next section.

Famine can still, however, be a significant tool for PRS in limited areas. Another common misconception is that famine is 'caused' by drought, floods or other natural disasters. Drought in Iowa and in Africa are quite different events and famines only occur where large numbers of people have already exhausted their reserves – of food, of money, of the human body. The early warning signs of famine are well known: sharply rising market prices for food, sales of jewellery and other stores of value, outmigration in search of work, consumption of foods not normally eaten.

When these signs are noted, it is important above all, *not* to intervene. At that point, too, a natural disaster can help to trigger a food crisis. So is it worth reflecting on ways to disorganise such possible precipitating factors as flood control or locust abatement. War, as we have seen, is another extremely effective tool for creating masses of vulnerable people.

Natural and man-made disasters displaced some 50 million people in 1996, either in their own countries or as cross-border refugees. Four-fifths of these people were wholly dependent on international aid for their survival. The economic costs of dealing with emergencies of all kinds was about $1 billion a year in the 1960s, $3 billion in the 1970s, $9 billion a year in the 1980s. The financial reckoning for the 1990s will be higher still.

Already the United Nations spends more than 50 per cent of its budget on emergency relief, as compared to 25 per cent in 1989. In the coming years, the task will be to discourage by all possible means – intellectual, political, physical – costly interventions to salvage unsalvageable people.

A further argument against 'humanitarian' aid in times of famine is supplied by the behaviour of local power elites. The better-off compatriots of the vulnerable can be counted upon to buttress our own Population Reduction Strategies and to discourage soft-hearted Northerners from pleading for relief. Landlords and merchants with grain reserves make fortunes in times of food crisis and are not going to give away their stores. Warlords may hold their own people hostage in order to attract humanitarian aid. When it arrives, they take control over it.

These faction leaders were once able to use one or the other of the Cold War powers for financing their expansionist activities. Now that this option has disappeared, they have discovered that famine and international compassion will serve just as well. Humanitarian agencies theoretically distributing the aid are not as free to succour the victims as they may appear. Even though they are particularly well placed to understand just how they are being used, these organisations are trapped. If they denounce the warlords, they will be forced to leave the country and the famine victims. If they don't, they give the local dictator international visibility and cloak him in a spurious legitimacy.

We recommend explaining to the public that to give such bribes to tinpot dictators is worse than giving nothing; that 'humanitarian' does not necessarily mean 'good'. Naturally, from the warlord's point of view, the famine – and thus the aid

– should last as long as possible. Our argument would be, rather, 'let's get it over with'.

IV. Pestilence

In *Revelation*, the Fourth Horseman is called simply Death but his 'pale horse' (in some translations 'pallid' or 'greenish') is the colour of decomposing corpses and 'Hell follows him' to swallow up the victims of plague. He is the most redoubtable and for our purposes, the most useful of the Horsemen. Historically, pandemics have had a far greater impact on population dynamics than war or even famine.

Pestilence unavoidably prunes live as well as dead wood; some who should be spared perish; disease does not always distinguish between rich and poor, competent and inept, useful and superfluous. Statistically speaking, however, it strikes the more vulnerable and dispensable first.

Throughout the contemporary world, in developed and Third World countries alike, life expectancies improve with income and education. In Britain, for all age groups, death rates have long been two to three times higher at the bottom of the social scale than at the top, a gap that widened further between 1981 and 1991. In the USA, states with the most unequal distribution of household income are also those with the highest death rates for heart disease, cancer and homicides.

Even during the Black Death, the rich found it easier to escape to the countryside than the indigent. When an epidemic of meningitis broke out in Brazil in 1974, wealthy Brazilians packed up and went abroad until it had run its course. As an Indian physician says, 'People who wear ties don't get cholera.'

Initially in colonial times and particularly after the Second World War, Western administrators introduced a few basic public health and sanitation measures to virgin Third World territory where people had for centuries pursued their high-fertility, high-mortality, disease-prone ways. Colonisers also brought new crops and improved agricultural systems so that food became more abundant. The impact was dramatic.

Such seemingly minor changes caused an unprecedented drop in mortality. Because fertility rates remained unchanged, often exceeding mortality rates by huge percentages, massive population increases ensued. In 1935, for example, the

British–administered Indian Ocean island of Mauritius had almost identical birth and death rates; by 1966, the birth rate was little higher than 30 years previously (36/1000 as compared to 31/1000) but the death rate had plummeted from 30/1000 to 9/1000 and the population had nearly doubled in 30 years.[15]

The history of the introduction of sanitation, hygiene and better diets in nineteenth-century England or turn-of-the-century New York confirms the disproportionate influence of simple measures on infant and child mortality in the South.

Such interventions were not unreservedly philanthropic. When plague struck British India, an all-out public health campaign was mounted. As soon as cases among the British were brought under control, funding and resources dried up, plague was declared 'endemic' in the native-born community and Indians were left worse off than before.

Ranking

Just as people of different classes inhabiting the same physical (national or even local) space can have widely differing health outcomes, so huge differences in the principle causes of death exist between rich and poor countries. One needs, however, to approach the figures with caution since underdeveloped countries routinely mislabel causes of death:

Table I Causes of death in 1990, by disease (000s)

Developed Countries		Developing Countries	
Cardiovascular	5245	Infectious/Parasitic	9166
Cancer	2413	Cardiovascular	9082
Injuries	834	Injuries	4251
Respiratory Infections	389	Respiratory Infections	3992
Diabetes	176	Cancer	3611
Infectious/Parasitic	163	Maternal/Perinatal	2812
Maternal/Perinatal	85	Nutritional Deficiencies	604
Nutritional Deficiencies	30	Diabetes	396

Source: British Medical Journal, Vol. 314, 10 May 1997, p. 1367 (Based on WHO).

The World Health Organisation (WHO) has supplied more recent figures for causes of death, although the breakdown is less precise.

Table II Causes of death in 1996, by disease (000s) and percentage

Developed Countries 12.116			Developing Countries 39.921		
Circulatory System	5.6	46%	Infectious/Parasitic	17.2	43%
Other, Unknown	2.8	23%	Circulatory System	9.6	24%
Malignant Neoplasm	2.5	21%	Perinatal/Maternal	4.4	11%
Chronic Pulmonary	0.97	8%	Malignant Neoplasms	4.0	10%
Perinatal, Maternal	0.12	1%	Other, Unknown	3.2	8%
Infectious, Parasitic	0.12	1%	Chronic, Pulmonary	2.0	5%

Source: WHO.

The huge *Global Burden of Disease (GBD)* study undertaken jointly by WHO, the Harvard School of Public Health and the World Bank has established the most refined and comprehensive set of figures we can hope for. The authors of the *GBD* foresee the following changes in the rank of 15 leading causes of the disease burden[16] (not the same as causes of death) between 1990 and 2020:

Table III Incidence of disease factors (world)

Disease or Injury	Rank 1990	Rank 2020
Lower Respiratory Infection	1	6
Diarrhoeal Diseases	2	9
Conditions Perinatal Period	3	11
Unipolar Major Depression	4	2
Coronary Heart Disease	5	1
Cerebrovascular Disease	6	4
Tuberculosis	7	7
Measles	8	25
Road Traffic Accidents	9	3
Congenital Anomalies	10	13
Malaria	11	25
Chronic Pulmonary Disease	12	5
Falls	13	19
Iron-deficiency Anaemia	14	39
Protein-Energy Malnutrition	15	37

Source: *The Global Burden of Disease*, Vol. I, p. 375.

Finally, it is interesting to look at causes of death from the lifestyle perspective. Once again, the WHO has the figures:

Table IV Deaths attributed to various risk factors, by rank [000s] 1990

Risk Factor	World	% Deaths	Developed	Delevoping
Malnutrition	5881	11.7	0	5881
Tobacco	3037	6	1577	1460
Hypertension	2918	5.8	1406	1512
Water/Sanit.	2668	5.3	35	2665
Physical Inactivity	1991	3.9	1099	892
Occupational	1129	2.2	230	899
Unsafe Sex	1094	2.2	87	1007
Alchool	773	1.5	136	637
Air Pollution	568	1.1	275	293
Illicit Drugs	100	0.2	38	62

Source: *The Global Burden of Disease*, Vol. I, Tables 6.2 to 6.12, pp. 311–15

These tables provide a rough guide for the areas of PRS emphasis that we recommend to the Commissioning Parties. We cannot provide detailed comments on all possible causes of death – the *GBD* team identifies 107 categories and sub-categories – but we can choose certain areas of particular significance for our own concerns.

The authors of *The Global Burden of Disease* propose a convenient codification of disease and death: Group I is composed of communicable, maternal, perinatal and nutritional conditions; Group II of non-communicable diseases and Group III of injuries (including self-inflicted ones) and accidents. In the developed world, 86 per cent of deaths are to be found in Group II, that of non-communicable illnesses. More surprisingly, as causes of death these diseases are also far more important than contagious diseases in many developing regions, including Latin America and especially China.

The findings of the *GBD* study warrant more detailed attention to lifestyle factors, particularly those relevant to heart disease and stroke.

Catering to smokers is one promising approach. Addiction is spreading fast in increasingly affluent Third World societies like

China and corporations are concentrating their advertising and promotion budgets in areas where the public is less hostile to their message. The World Bank suggests that perhaps 2 million smoking-related deaths a year will be the norm in the first decade of the coming century. WHO sees the tobacco epidemic causing more premature deaths and disability in 2020 than any single disease, particularly in China and the former socialist economies, but also in the developed countries.

Mortality from polluted water and poor sanitation, domestic and personal hygiene ought to increase as well. We devote a short section to water issues later. Other bad personal habits – lack of physical activity, unsafe sex, alcohol and drugs contributed a further 3,250,000 deaths, 80 per cent of them in the developing regions. The *Global Burden* authors also confidently predict a rise in car accidents, self-inflicted injuries, violence and casualties from war.

Group I causes of mortality comprising communicable, perinatal, maternal and nutritional conditions are clearly most promising for our purposes. Particular scope is afforded by the range of infectious/parasitic diseases to which, in 1996, the WHO attributed over 17 million deaths. Maternal and perinatal mortality also hold potential.

In our review of famine, we stressed the importance of limiting food availability even though relatively few people die directly from hunger. This is confirmed in Table IV which cites malnutrition as the decisive factor in 11.7 per cent of all deaths. Anti-food strategies still contribute strongly to the grand design of population reduction because malnutrition and hunger prepare the favourable terrain for illness and epidemics.

The Tide of History

The goal of PRS is broader than merely reducing aggregate numbers, however ambitious this is in itself. One must further seek to revert to pre-colonial conditions in the South and, even more difficult, to a pre-Enlightenment mentality in the North. The myth, indeed the cult, of inexorable progress must be abandoned.

After two centuries of medical advances, particularly since the advent of antibiotics after the Second World War, people have come to assume that every disease has a cure. The plain truth is that many no longer do. Resistant parasites, bacteria and viruses are in many cases outstripping medicine's capacity to cope. Medical science cannot accomplish miracles and must continue to focus its attention on those groups and geographical areas where it remains possible to hold the Grim Reaper at bay.

Science and medicine must practise worldwide the *triage* method, invented by First World War surgeons who shunted the hopeless cases aside so as to concentrate on the soldiers who could be saved. It is normal that the diseases receiving most attention should be those which afflict groups best able to support the costs of complex research and pay for quality care. Meanwhile, the public in the North, but more particularly in the South, must learn greater fatalism in the face of disease and bow to the inevitable, just as people did for centuries.

On the other hand, 'scapegoating' is a natural tendency which can be discreetly fostered. Since ancient Athens, every epidemic has been blamed on some despised group such as minorities or 'impure elements', often women. Plague-stricken societies may also readily believe themselves to be objects of divine retribution against the spiritual deficiencies of their leaders or perhaps victims of plots fomented by powerful foreigners. One should be prepared to exploit such suspicions and divisions.

Urbanisation, overcrowding and poor sanitation will continue to provide the favourable terrain for the spread of disease. Africa is the least urbanised of the poor continents yet even there 30 per cent of the population already lives in cities and more people are drawn to them every day. To make the most of this context, we specifically recommend full privatisation of public services, especially sewage disposal, waste treatment, water provision and rubbish collection.

The World Bank and the IMF have been in the forefront of the transfer of public services to the private sector. In practice, the Bank's policies now have far more influence on health in the underdeveloped world than either the World Health Organisation or local health ministries, both of which have lost ground and initiative. As the Bank has pointed out, health risks among the poor, including 'poor sanitation, unsafe water supplies, poor personal and food hygiene, inadequate garbage disposal, indoor air pollution and crowded and inferior housing' are collectively associated with one-third of the 'global burden of disease'.

The Bank's solution is that governments 'provide a regulatory and administrative framework within which efficient and accountable providers (often in the private sector) have an incentive to offer households the services they want and *are willing to pay for*, including water supply, sanitation, garbage collection, clean-burning stoves and housing'.[17]

Experience shows, however, that when these services must be paid for at their real economic cost and supply a profit as well, they are placed well beyond the reach of slum-dwellers and poor neighbourhoods, thereby encouraging vectors of disease. One can acquire only a certain degree of immunity to open drains, tainted water and rats. The Bank's market approach to health care is now dominant and it should finish the job of privatising medicine wherever that process is not yet completed, taking as its guide the US model, and adapting it for each country.

In any event, nations undergoing structural adjustment cannot afford free health care. Since India first signed up for structural adjustment in the early 1990s, its health budget (excluding minimal funds for AIDS) has been amputated by 30 per cent, repeating the experience of country after country. Whereas malaria is blossoming in India as never before, the anti-malaria programme has been cut by over 40 per cent.

As their public service budgets are slashed, governments must sooner or later arrive at a fee-paying system and eradicate the notion among their citizens that health care is somehow a right. People must learn to be clients or contributing members of collective health insurance, not passive beneficiaries of public dispensing machines.

New possibilities for synergy should be exploited. For example, World Bank engineering and agricultural projects may contribute to malaria as they have done in India by creating stagnant pools or marshy areas which make excellent mosquito breeding grounds. All environment-related diseases which cannot be successfully addressed at the individual level will be enhanced by privatisation.

The decline of health budgets and the nature of the world market, including the health care market, should cause qualified medical personnel to seek opportunities abroad. Thirty thousand Africans and vast numbers of Indians, Pakistanis and other Asian doctors have already done so. Standard structural adjustment packages include currency devaluations which make imported drugs and hospital equipment more expensive. Generic drugs which could reduce costs to patients should be discouraged on the rational grounds that companies that do not profit from their old drugs will cease to invest in research on desperately needed new ones.

Privatisation of public services, medical practice, health facilities and pharmaceuticals will help but cannot do the whole job. Many urban neighbourhoods and most villages lack such amenities altogether, paid or otherwise. Here the preferred strategy would consist in blocking low-tech, low-cost interventions which some of the more effective development agencies have pioneered. Most public health breakthroughs, such as smallpox eradication or widespread childhood vaccination, have been brought about not so much by governments as by the international brigades of UNICEF or the WHO.

However difficult it may be to discredit the UN specialised agency for children, UNICEF must be recognised as a formidable foe in the fight for population reduction. Northern government contributions will need to be discouraged (already under way in the United States and Japan). The financial accounts of field staff should be examined with a magnifying glass so as to uncover and highlight possible fraudulent or wasteful practices. A media campaign on the theme 'Where does your Christmas card money *really* go?', placing the least favourable light on the agency's practices and administrative expenditures, could be beneficial.

UNICEF stresses immunisation, oral rehydration salts for diarrhoea-stricken babies and cheap antibiotic treatments for fighting common infections. It claims to prevent 5 million deaths a year and asserts that with better coverage, a further 8 million could be avoided. Unconventional methods may be necessary to disrupt or, better still, halt the activities of UNICEF and a few effective non-governmental organisations like OXFAM in target countries. We would not entirely rule out the use of infiltrators, sabotage, disruption and selective attacks on personnel in order to discourage existing staff, staff candidates and volunteers but these should be used only as a last resort.

Other Troops

The MEDFLAG programmes which the United States Army carried out in Ghana, Côte D'Ivoire and Botswana in 1994 and 1995 have wisely been discontinued. These health 'blitzkriegs', undertaken in cooperation with local military and health personnel were immensely popular with the public, media and government. They brought large teams of medical combat specialists to each country for three weeks to supply medical and veterinary services in urban and rural areas, deploy large-scale inoculation programmes against prevalent local diseases and train local medical personnel to cope with health emergencies and disasters. In the bargain, they provided valuable *in situ* training for the US personnel and whipped disparate non-governmental organisations into shape to cooperate with health objectives fixed by local authorities.

Careful coordination with these authorities before and during MEDFLAG exercises reduced suspicion and changed attitudes towards the USA and towards the military in general. If such operations were to be generalised in Africa and elsewhere, they could seriously threaten PRS. We note with satisfaction that the Pentagon no longer seems to take an interest in such programmes and has redeployed the medical units concerned to Eastern Europe.[18]

Concentrating national health budgets on clinical medicine and hospital 'cures' rather than on prevention will produce a similar effect. Most Third World governments need little urging in this direction and have for years targeted health spending to the more prosperous classes of their own societies. The rich have access to modern hospital facilities while elsewhere in rundown rural and neighbourhood clinics, hypodermic needles are reused and simple lab tests cannot be run. Public hospitals may themselves be the most efficient disease vectors one could imagine.

Whatever critics claim, it does no good to complain that primary health care for the poor 'should' replace tertiary care for the rich, just as it is utopian to pretend, as the WHO does, that 'Health for All' is attainable in our time or any other.

These naive assertions take no account of market economics nor of the balance of power among institutions. The WHO's own definition of 'health' is itself so broad as to be virtually meaningless: 'Health is a state of complete physical, mental and social well-being and not merely the absence of disease or infirmity.' Compared to this all-encompassing definition, the bleating utopianism of the Universal Declaration of Human Rights seems positively restrictive! We doubt that anyone could honestly claim to be 'healthy' according to the WHO's lights.

Even when more strictly defined, health is costly and growing more so. In 1990, according to the World Bank, public and private expenditures on formal health services reached an unprecedented $1,700 billion, representing fully 8 per cent of world product. Ninety per cent of that amount was spent in the rich countries where less than 20 per cent of the world population lives. The remaining 10 per cent will be increasingly devoted to Third World elites who can afford to pay their share of world health expenditure. There is no reason why these proportions should change substantially in years to come.

We have stressed that infectious and parasitic disease cannot remain entirely confined to poor countries and poor neighbourhoods. Spillovers will necessarily occur. Although 'Third World diseases' will claim a few lives in the West, they are vital adjuncts to the pruning process. The occasional, isolated and exotic fatality in Los Angeles or London will also keep the fright factor vivid and reinforce the civilised/barbarian dichotomy. The real threat to rich countries is of a different order.

Superbugs

The WHO requires national reporting of only three diseases, all of them tropical: cholera, plague and yellow fever. These hardly qualify as clear and present dangers for Northerners. The seemingly more protected countries must, however, cope with their own characteristic maladies. We are not referring to heart disease, obesity and other afflictions of affluence but to the threatening emergence of 'superbugs'.

These mutant strains have waxed and flourished from decades of feeding on a rich diet of antibiotics. A few microbes now actually thrive on them; they are addicted and literally cannot live without the medicines initially developed to kill them. The discovery that a poison can become a food is especially alarming because the 'food' involved is the last resort antibiotic, vancomycin. Resistance to this erstwhile microbe killer can and does jump from one pathogen to another, for instance *enterococcus* has transferred its vancomycin resistance to *staphylococcus*.

Staph bacteria are the leading cause of hospital infections and super-resistant staph *aureus* has already been discovered in Japanese, British and US hospitals. When many people with impaired immunity are concentrated in one spot, as they are in hospitals, superbugs have a field day. No one has yet tallied their devastating impact precisely, because assigning a proximate cause for the deaths of already sick patients is problematic.

Not all infectious agents have mutated to the point of devouring antibiotics for nourishment. However, as in the case of genetically manipulated crops, too many policy-makers and scientists who should know better proceed as if Darwin had never existed, as if life-forms were somehow static and immutable. To the contrary, natural selection embraces all life-forms including the lowliest, whose brief lifespans and rapid reproduction allow them to mutate much faster than more sophisticated organisms.

According to the WHO, antibiotics, 'used by too many people to treat the wrong kind of infections at the wrong dosage and for the wrong period of time' are the chief reason for the proliferation of drug-resistant strains. Other studies tend to show that cost-cutting measures in hospitals also help to ensure a build-up of microbial resistance when doses are inadequate and antibiotics are used one after the other rather than in association. Whatever its origins, the phenomenon of increasing microbial resistance is beyond question.

Natural selection of these pathogens is itself speeding up because it no longer depends on random genetic advantage alone. Some microbes are now actually programmed to mutate under stress. Some display collective behaviours conducive to group survival. Others 'scour their environments for potentially useful genetic material' to be found in bits of DNA called 'plasmids' or 'transposons' which may then confer resistance to dozens of drugs.[19]

Conventional cleanliness is no protection either: plenty of germs have learned to love soap, disinfectant, acid and high temperatures. To fight the new invaders, few drugs are being developed or licensed, especially if the illnesses they might combat are more or less confined to poor countries and poor neighbourhoods where profits are hard to come by. At the same time that resistant pathogens are proliferating, the development of new antimicrobial drugs has slowed dramatically, largely because the cost of bringing a new antibiotic from lab bench to market can reach $350 million.[20]

The antibiotic market is likely to be worth $40 billion in the year 2000. The more the phenomenon of resistance to tried-and-true antibiotics spreads, the more differentiated rich–poor health care will become, since a day's treatment of the latest superbug with the latest superdrug can easily cost $500. Such costs reflect the companies' right to amortise their research and hedge their risks, particularly since many drugs are similar and competition to market them is fierce. Japan's 43,000 drug salesmen call on Japanese doctors more than once a day on average. (British GPs get off more easily with an average of 62 visits a year.)

Drug companies and physicians need to police themselves. Too often, in too many places, physicians prescribe 'last resort' drugs as 'first resort' medication or use broad-spectrum, expensive antimicrobials to treat common infections like sinusitis. Companies make broad-spectrum claims for their antibiotics that no substance could possibly live up to.

Drugs banned in Europe or the USA are routinely unloaded elsewhere. Antibiotics are incorporated in medicinal cocktails where they have no business (for instance, anti-diarrhoeals). Physicians receive 'incentive' kickbacks which encourage them to prescribe drug X rather than drug Y. Between the manufacturing source and a sales subsidiary of the same company, the cost of a drug may increase manyfold. Such practices are common.

As bacterial resistance increases – and the number of ways bacteria acquire resistance to antimicrobial drugs is astonishing – illness becomes less and less amenable to treatment. And as the public in rich countries begins to understand the reasons for the resistance phenomenon and its consequences for their own health, pharmaceutical companies – and possibly even doctors – will be pilloried. Once again we are forced to 'diagnose' a mercantile sector which takes little interest in, or care of, the system that sustains it. Drug companies sorely need internal checks.

Commonplace Plagues

We shall now undertake a brief inventory, examining from highest to lowest the diseases we expect to contribute most to Third World mortality (AIDS being in a class by itself). The spectacular new and new-old diseases which have lately figured prominently in the headlines are far from being the biggest killers. A single case of infection with an exotic virus like Ebola, Lassa or Marburg may be enough to provoke panic and attention from Hollywood but for purposes of PRS, the real news is elsewhere.

Tuberculosis

The deadliest diseases are actually to be found among the new-old standbys. Tuberculosis, known since ancient times, is rapidly developing lethal, multidrug-resistant strains. Overall, it killed more than 3 million people in 1995. Its mortality potential and preferred target groups make it a remarkably promising population reduction tool for the future.

As the disease gains in prevalence and severity, society may decide that infected people must be forcibly restrained and made to take their medicine or even incarcerated like New York's 'Typhoid Mary', the bacillus-carrying cook arrested in 1907 and detained for most of her life. If the New York TB caseload continues to grow (4,000 in 1994 with a high proportion in Harlem) it is sure to provoke a higher degree of social control. Already New York patients who skip medical examination appointments or refuse to take their medicine can be arrested.

Severe quarantine measures may be reintroduced ('quarantina' means '40 days') to prevent contagion, particularly at national borders. Coercive measures would weaken the 'individual human rights' approach to patients in favour of community survival which is precisely the type of mentality we seek to encourage.

Among the many advantages of tuberculosis as a population-pruning tool, we may mention the following.

- TB, even in its newly resistant forms, seems to have lost its power to shock. Although it was once responsible for one European death in seven, it is now associated in people's minds mainly with nineteenth-century operatic heroines expiring in garrets.

- Health experts estimate that $100 million a year would be necessary to mount an effective global assault on TB. The disease now attracts a mere $16 million in international funds for eradication and treatment.

- The BCG vaccine still works for about two-thirds of the Northern children to whom it is administered, but field trials in Africa have shown that it confers no protection at all there, probably because the subjects harbour other bacteria not present in the North. This leaves the South open to the disease without any vaccine at all.

- In the North, many networks of sanatoria and clinics were dismantled in the 1970s since TB was thought to be a thing of the past. In the South, people who receive medication for TB frequently stop taking it as soon as they feel better, allowing them both to infect others and to contribute to increased resistance of the bacilli.

- Diagnosis is slow: lab tests can require up to one month to identify normal TB and two months for more elusive drug resistant forms. By that time, the carrier has already passed his infection on.

- The disease, especially in its more virulent guises, has a particular affinity for undesirable populations: HIV carriers are extremely susceptible and TB is now the leading killer of AIDS patients. In the ex-Soviet Union, it is rife among prisoners and former prisoners who are infected by the thousands. Low-income populations of New York and London have significant levels of TB incidence. Refugees are at high risk since they move about and, even when properly diagnosed, rarely complete the treatment.

- Treatment is costly. According to the WHO, in the United States the approximate cost of treating a TB outpatient is $2000 while state-of-the-art treatment of a multidrug-resistant strain may reach an astronomical $250,000. The identity of the patients (AIDS sufferers, prisoners, inner-cities denizens) is likely to dissuade society from investing such sums for very much longer.

Paradoxically, the WHO affirms that, in the Third World at least, individual TB sufferers *could* be cured with $13 worth of drugs. But in these countries, less than 0.2 per cent of all health expenditure is devoted to TB even though it is frequently a leading cause of death. Only a minuscule 0.4 per cent of foreign aid to Third World health goes to TB. In dozens of poor countries, the WHO also notes 'disruptions in the supply of anti-TB medicines. These disruptions are a sure way to encourage the spread of multidrug-resistant strains of TB.'

Given all these factors militating in favour of increasingly rampant infection, we see tuberculosis as a precious adjunct to any PRS. Not only is TB research and action pitifully funded but the longer the epidemic is neglected the more difficult and costly it will become to act when societies finally take notice. TB deaths worldwide were up 13 per cent between 1994 and 1995 alone. Co-infection between HIV and TB and the synergies described above are likely to keep these percentages climbing at similar or higher rates.

Malaria

The second Third World rank for mortality is shared by AIDS and malaria, another ancient scourge. Like TB, malaria has developed particularly vicious, drug-resistant strains. Massive spraying with DDT and other potent insecticides resulted in the selection of super-resistant anopheles mosquitoes whose bites transmit the four different kinds of plasmodium parasites that infect 300 to 500 million people and kill nearly 3 million a year. And again like TB, the initial, substantial drop in incidence created a false sense of security in the 1970s. The number of plasmodium carriers was reduced to 4 or 5 million worldwide and complacency gave the parasites a chance to gain the upper hand once more.

At the beginning of the 1990s, health workers in Indochina were confronted for the first time with a malarial strain resistant to all known therapies. The same is now true in parts of Gabon and Kenya as well. Resistance is gaining ground elsewhere in Africa, India and Latin America and malarial zones are spreading due to global warming. Forty per cent of the world's population lives in a high-risk zone.

Spraying is no longer feasible and today any meaningful programme of control and 'best practice' action would need to be universal, internationally coordinated by the WHO and generously financed. Many of the factors we noted for TB also make malaria a useful population inhibitor, with the additional advantage that it strikes far fewer Westerners than inhabitants of the tropics. For our purposes, however, reduction or elimination of financing is practically all that is needed because so many therapeutic avenues are already largely blocked.

Pharmaceutical companies are notoriously unwilling to invest in drug research for poverty-stricken zones. New anti-malarial drugs tend in any case to become rapidly inoperative: the efficacy of the last highly touted one lasted about three years. The curative-preventive drug, mefloquine, produces grave and debilitating side-effects in many patients and such new drugs will also, in time, encourage resistance. Interest currently centres on nitric oxides and on cocktails of anti-malarials with antibiotics.

A Chinese herbal compound made from wormwood and the Indian neem tree also seem to have promising anti-malarial properties but herbal remedies receive meagre research funding because they cannot be patented and made profitable. A Colombian physician has developed a vaccine for which he claims 36–55 per cent efficacy but he has given the formula and legal rights to the WHO rather than selling them to a corporation, so it will not be developed unless public funding is forthcoming.

The only quasi-permanent remedy is likely to be found in various forms of environmental control (such as introduction of fish and other natural predators to feed on mosquitoes and larvae) but research in this area has barely begun. The current outlook for curbing, much less eradicating, malaria seems doomed.

This being the case, aside from letting nature take its course, we recommend stressing the dangers of travel. The Thai–Burmese border is already a 'no-go' for Westerners because it is the epicentre of resistant malaria which has already spread to northern Thailand, much of Cambodia and Burma. To make it spread more rapidly, refugee camps in the area should be dismantled so that the plasmodium can go back on the road. The mosquito itself does not need to travel; the transmission belt works through infected human carriers of resistant parasites who are then bitten again.

US soldiers should be kept out of malarial danger zones. Every time a GI gets the disease, the American army steps up its investments in malaria research. Without this American interest, funding would be even lower than it is and progress towards possible new remedies considerably retarded.

Exotica

What are the prospects for the 'exotica'? In just a few years, isolated outbreaks, terrifying symptoms and talented writers have turned once obscure pathologies like 'Ebola' into household names. As PRS, we expect relatively little of these 'hot zone' resident viruses, whether filoviruses (vector unknown, possibly bats or monkeys: Ebola, Marburg, Reston), arenaviruses (spread by rodents: Machupo, Choriomeningitis, Haemorrhagic fever, Lassa fever) or bunyaviruses (spread by ticks: Crimean Congo and Renal Syndrome haemorrhagic fevers). Precisely because they are so spectacular, these outbreaks have been closely monitored and, so far at least, rapidly circumscribed.

Cultural practices non-existent in the West encourage contagion. In most African societies physical contact with the dead is expected and corpses must be purified by washing and by the expulsion of urine and faeces, practically ensuring viral transmission to family and other mourners. We do not discount the possibility of a deadly virus carrier taking a plane to New York or Paris, but we do not see these diseases as perpetrators of mass mortality. The dreaded Ebola, for example, is extremely sensitive to ultraviolet light. Naturally, if these exotic viruses become widespread enough to mutate rapidly, the consequences would be unpredictable.

In one way, however, the onset of a terrifying and exceptional disease can encourage mortality beyond the virus's own physical capacity to destroy. From long experience and for good reasons, Westerners have grown used to high professional standards and selfless dedication on the part of their doctors and nurses and tend to assign automatically such altruistic behaviour to medical workers everywhere. They should think again.

When in 1994 plague (*yersinia pestis*) struck Surat in Western India, three-quarters of the private doctors in the city fled and only a small fraction of hospital staff reported for duty. One hundred patients suffering from the plague who had turned up at the local hospital saw that no medical help was available, thought better of their decision and went home, spreading the disease as they went. The military had to be called in to keep the other patients inside the hospital to prevent further contagion. The behaviour of the medical profession in some instances may actually contribute to the spread of disease.

Old Standbys

Infant and child mortality can be enhanced by bottle-feeding. In the Third World, breast milk substitutes guarantee that a high proportion of babies thus fed will not get a proper ration (too expensive) and will be drinking impure water from unsterilised bottles and teats.

Airborne respiratory diseases like drug-resistant pneumonia are returning; so are others like measles (a million deaths yearly) and whooping cough (300,000). With rapidly mutating viruses all around us, one cannot discount the possibility of another 'Spanish' flu (which actually came from Asia). In 1917–18, it brought down 25 million people, three times the number killed in the butchery of the First World War.

Among the water-borne diseases, diarrhoea is most basic and reliable. In the absence of oral rehydration, it can carry off small children in a matter of hours and usually wipes out two and a half million children a year plus half a million adults. Some 80 million people are now exposed to endemic cholera.

A few diseases are rapidly regressing, among them leprosy and Guinea worm. The WHO thinks it can eradicate polio by 2005 although wars, poor quality vaccines and lack of cold storage to preserve them may cause it to miss its target. There are still 100,000 polio cases a year.

These minor and partial successes can be easily thwarted through the intensification of conflict and crowding. Any local conflict is a plus for PRS because it will complicate the day-today operations of public health agencies, making their inter-ventions more difficult and dangerous. Whatever measures reduce substantial areas of the globe to no-man's-lands will necessarily stimulate mortality.

Violence in Algeria has closed down clinics and made public health practices like vaccinations problematic. Child mortality has increased there for the first time after 20 years of falling rates. The hell-hole of the African Great Lakes region, full of refugees and other fallout from the Rwanda massacres is a case study of violence and chaos as the best vectors of disease, from measles to malaria. Innumerable corpses were thrown into Lake Kivu from which people then drank the water. The result was 50,000 cholera victims.

In case anyone doubted it, it has now been scientifically shown by a UN 'Habitat' study that 'intensity of exposure' – children sleeping together or sharing their lodgings with domestic animals like pigs – will increase disease incidence far beyond what could be expected from poor sanitation alone. The intensity factor counts for TB, measles, whooping cough and diarrhoea, all of which spread more quickly and kill more often in overcrowded homes and neighbourhoods.

AIDS

Whatever the manifold possibilities of TB, malaria, exotic or old standby diseases, AIDS will change the face of humanity far more than any of them. Although not yet the planet's principal killer, AIDS is already making an uncommon contribution to mortality rates, mostly in the South. Indeed, the Acquired Immune Deficiency Syndrome is acquired less and less frequently in the North. Over 90 per cent of all new cases occur in the Third World, three-quarters of them in Africa.

How many people have AIDS? In mid-1997, the official number of cases *reported* to the World Health Organisation was a ludicrous 1.65 million. The UN Programme on HIV/AIDS esti-mated the true number of virus carriers in 1996 at 30.6 million, with 16,000 new infections occurring daily or 5.8 million yearly. Here is an unprecedented ally for PRS: yearly increases of 19 per cent, more than two-thirds of them in Sub-Saharan Africa and 22 per cent in Asia. New infections are concentrated among young people between 15 and 24 years; 10 per cent are children.

Close to 12 million people have already died of AIDS, four-fifths of them in Africa. More important, mortality figures are making giant strides: AIDS deaths in 1997 will represent fully a fifth of all AIDS deaths since the beginning of the epidemic, half as many again as in 1996. The numbers are all on the side of wildfire propagation.

Such are the figures. The sociology of AIDS also works to the benefit of PRS. Official and religious attitudes towards sexuality continue to encourage the spread of AIDS. Prudish public administrations refuse to acknowledge that widespread homosexuality, extramarital sex, prostitution, promiscuous behaviour and drug addiction can exist in their societies.

Whether in Muslim countries, China, Japan, Russia, India or Africa, the predictable reactions of mass denial and the conviction that 'It can't happen here' delay popular education and prevention measures. The disease has time to set down deep roots.

Muslim clerics proclaim that Islamic values will protect people and that those who get the disease get exactly what they deserve. According to some clergy, such people should be shunned. A Mufti in Dubai cites the Prophet's advice on infectious diseases: 'Run away from them as you would run from a lion' and opines that 'Those who are infected with this virus (except those who acquired it through no fault of their own) are at war with God and the Prophet and are being punished for their sins. They should therefore be avoided at all costs.'

Like the Catholic priesthood, Muslim clerics cannot encourage condoms which they believe encourage people to indulge in 'free sex'. Another Islamic scholar says, 'AIDS patients are neither curable nor of any use to society except for spreading this dreadful disease. They should be put in a separate village, like the village for lepers.'[21]

Prevention is neglected, either because of the 'denial syndrome' or simply because heavily indebted governments have no money for education campaigns. As for cure, treating one African patient costs as much as educating ten primary school children for a year. In Zimbabwe, where perhaps 900 people die weekly from AIDS, the government has cut off expensive treatments like kidney dialysis because it cannot afford to spend scarce cash on the dying.

Individual culture works in favour of the virus as well, particularly macho attitudes. In Africa, men sneer at condoms, often citing the maxim, 'You don't take a shower with a raincoat on.' In French-speaking Africa, the acronym SIDA becomes 'Syndrome Imaginaire pour Décourager les Amoureux', an invention of the 'whites' to discourage African sexuality.

Elsewhere, especially in the countryside, the viral, or even physical origins of the disease, are not necessarily acknowledged: sometimes it is transmitted by the 'night people' or 'witches' and can be prevented by observing prescribed rites and customs. The notion that the only way to prevent AIDS is to change sexual behaviour is far from universal in Africa or in the rest of the Third World.

Women in many societies are frequently dependent on men for survival and lack control over their sexual partners, including their husbands, who demand unprotected sex even though they consort with prostitutes outside marriage. Most infected women in Arab societies have been infected by their husbands. In more extreme cases, women may be obliged to take up prostitution to survive. Female sex workers are obviously most at risk since they are usually in no position to insist on safe sex. Truck routes in Africa have been famous breeding grounds since the mid-1980s.

Only a few years after the virus was first detected in India in the early 1990s, this country now has more AIDS cases (over 3 million) than any other. Three million out of a total population of 950 million may seem insignificant but experts foresee at least 10, perhaps as many as 20 to 50 million virus carriers by the beginning of the next century when India will be the world centre of AIDS.

Part of the credit will go to its 5 million truck drivers (who average 150–200 sexual encounters with different women and girls a year) and its 10 million prostitutes. One hundred thousand of them work as 'cage girls' in Bombay's notorious Falkland Road red light district. More than half already carry HIV. Here too, the epidemic is beginning to reach into homes and touch women who claim that they have had sex with no one but their husbands.

In every country, in a longer or shorter time, however and wherever the epidemic may begin, it eventually gravitates to the most marginal and despised groups in the society. In Brazil, an epidemic which started with cocaine-snorting, partner-swapping jet-setters now rages in the *favelas*. In Africa, elites were also the first to be infected but the disease is moving down-market. New AIDS victims are no longer to be found among wealthy US homosexuals but in inner cities.

And so it goes: AIDS is an ideal PRS because it satisfies a desire for retribution against 'sinners' and it burns off the dross of society. An Indian intellectual told a Western reporter investigating AIDS in Bombay that AIDS will benefit the country because it will 'depopulate the vast underclass'. This mentality, which could not be more apt for our purposes, can be encouraged well beyond caste-ridden societies like India's. Everywhere the disease's victims seem 'to have brought it on themselves' and these victims will eventually become concentrated in the lowest social strata.

Among the killer diseases, AIDS research has been remarkably well funded, largely because of the pressure that its initial, well-organised US sufferers brought to bear on the federal government. The US AIDS research budget went from zero in 1982 to $1.4 billion in 1996. Thousands of scientists are studying HIV and its associated syndromes; many now speak of a cure, or at least a means of keeping the virus under control for years, so long as patients follow a strict regimen.

But at what cost? A year's triple-therapy treatment at current prices costs a minimum of $10,000 to $15,000 in the United States, so that even there it is inaccessible for many HIV positive people without health insurance. The manufacturers of AIDS drugs (Merck, Abbott, Roche, Glaxo Wellcome) point out that drug therapy costs far less than caring for a patient dying of AIDS. This is true: annual hospital care in the United States would cost a minimum of $60,000.

Treatment will remain completely beyond the reach of virtually all Third World patients. India's national AIDS budget is a paltry $20 million, about two cents per person. As for unprotected sex, cost will again be a determinant. The WHO estimated that condoms could cost the Third World agencies which buy them up to $1.3 billion for the decade 1995–2005. They are nowhere close to finding that kind of money.

Meanwhile, ethical purists oppose large-scale clinical vaccine or drugs trials in poor countries on grounds that some participants will receive placebos. Precisely because infection is so dense in Sub-Saharan Africa, researchers could study enough subjects to get significant results in a much shorter time than it would take them in developed countries. They also want to test the effect of different remedies on 'naive' patients who have never received any treatment and have not developed drug resistance.

The ethicists also claim that poor people will not benefit from the drugs that they risked their health to test. As soon as the trials are finished, their supplies of drugs will be cut off unless they can pay the market price, so trials should not take place at all among these populations. Unless a clinical protocol is suitable for Westerners, it should not, they say, be applied to Third World subjects.

For our purposes, we side with the ethicists: slower, more costly testing will buy time for the spread of AIDS. The virus will flourish not just among placebo subjects but among all the people who might otherwise have received effective therapy. It costs over $500 million to bring a new AIDS drug to the market.

As for contamination of undesirable populations in the wealthier countries, infected needles seem the shortest and most efficient route. The USA still has an estimated 1–2 million intravenous drug users, few of whom have access to clean needles. Two hundred thousand addicts live in New York alone and half of them tested HIV positive in 1995. A study in one Ukrainian city showed that infection rates among injecting drug users went from 5 per cent to 60 per cent in a single year.

Politicians are loath to fund needle exchange programmes for fear of campaign ads on television: picture of heroin addict shooting up with voice-over: 'This is how Mr X spent your tax dollars.' Where needle exchange programmes have been paid for, as in Britain, the Netherlands and even Kathmandu, they have demonstrably stabilised HIV infection among drug addicts.

We believe that AIDS will be a determining factor in PRS and in the existential shift of 'biopolitics' from concern with the (statistical) well-being of a given population to the pruning of a pestilential underclass. The 'sovereign' need not be concerned with the individual bodies of the members of this class since their own sexuality will condemn them to death in the most cost-effective manner.

As the disease moves inexorably down the social scale, the 'biopolitician' will learn that few votes are garnered by funding programmes for the dregs of humanity. Compassion for scum may be a virtue, illustrated by Mother Teresa, but it remains a heroic one. Happily, few politicians are heroes.

2.4

Prevention

Conquest, War, Famine and Pestilence have served to prune the human race time out of mind and have lost none of their relevance in our own day. We have attempted to show how they could be adapted to modern circumstances.

We now turn to Population Reduction Strategies which Saint John and Malthus could never have conceived because they are preventive and depend on late twentieth-century politics and technology, two aspects which cannot be separated entirely. Whereas Malthus saw no alternative to reliance on 'moral restraint', today's preventive PRS have as much, perhaps more, potential for reducing overall human numbers as the curative ones already described. This chapter concerns the possibilities offered by Reproductive Inhibition/Inhibitors, as we will call them (abbreviated to RI).

Fertilia and Sterilia

Let us begin with a parable. Two countries, Fertilia and Sterilia, have similar histories of colonialism, comparable populations and identical fertility rates when they gain independence in the late 1950s. In both countries, mortality rates have already been drastically curbed thanks to the spread of medical knowledge and basic hygiene.[1]

Post-colonial Sterilia is governed by an outward-looking commercial and trading class who immediately proclaim a high priority family planning programme, give it plenty of institutional support and create material incentives for people to participate. Safe abortion and sterilisation are available on demand and contraceptives are distributed free by strategically placed health centres. Children born are wanted and cherished.

Fertilia on the other hand is ostensibly run by large landowners but the power behind the throne is a traditionalist clergy whose view is that nature should take its course, which it naturally does. Predictably, four decades after independence, Fertilia's working-age population is four times what it used to be. With all those children to raise, it would be hard enough under any circumstances to improve the *status quo*, but a far larger volume of savings is needed in Fertilia than in Sterilia merely to maintain the previous standard of living.

If population is growing at 2 per cent a year and people are to continue to live as well, each year must also bring 2 per cent more schools, hospitals, teachers, doctors, equipment in each industry, jobs in each occupation, and so on. Nothing of the kind occurs. Farmland, in particular, has stubbornly refused to expand at the rate of 2 per cent per year, resulting in chronic rural unemployment and mass migration to the crime-ridden capital city. People spend what little income they have on immediate survival. Not only are savings low but the government's tax revenues are paltry, so it can afford few investments in infrastructure. Schools have long since given up trying to spread even basic literacy and girls are scarcely educated at all. Fertilia can no longer produce enough crops to feed all its people and has been forced to import more food each year. It bears a heavy foreign debt burden. Life is a mess.

Sterilia has kept its school-age population stable and improved its educational system enormously since the colonisers departed. People are literate and competent and they can take on a variety of reasonably complex jobs; this applies equally to women who have attended school and have no more children than they want. Savings and investment have allowed for modernisation, proper health care and infrastructure improvements. People in the countryside either have decently paid agricultural jobs or own their own farms. Food production is not a problem. Rural to urban migration is moderate and the city scene is manageable. Life may not be paradise, but it certainly beats Fertilia.

We end the morality tale here. Were it to continue, it would also recount that in Fertilia, disease is rife. Imported food is expensive, so poor people are frequently famished and malnourished. Some day soon, Fertilia will probably try to invade Sterilia, steal its assets and enslave or massacre its people; because the one investment the Fertilian state has made is in its army. Its masses of jobless and disaffected young people will be happy to oblige the leadership when conscripted – at least that way they will be fed.

Third World Sterilias, as we know, are rare. Our goal as a Working Party, and we assume it is the goal of the Commissioning Parties as well, is to improve the quality of life throughout the world, help countries to become more like Sterilia and thus preserve the free market which will otherwise be swamped by the proliferating Fertilian masses.

If life *is* to be improved, the corrective Population Reduction Strategies we have identified – the Horsemen – will not suffice. Reproduction will also need to be coaxed and coerced into patterns more conducive to a civilised existence.

Reproductive Arithmetic

Let us first examine the arithmetic contours of the problem. Thirty years ago, a mere 10 per cent of married couples in the Third World used some form of contraception.[2] Now the figure is said to be approaching 60 per cent, yet population growth has pursued the catastrophic curve we have already described.

The reasons for this sad state of affairs are economic, political, social and cultural; that is, complex. It is, however, entirely possible to act decisively in the area of Reproductive Inhibition because today, in the Third World:

- 120 million couples who claim they want to space or stop having children are not using any form of RI;

- 300 million additional couples are using RI methods which they themselves consider unsatisfactory or unreliable, resulting in an estimated 30 million unwanted pregnancies yearly;

- an average 40–45 million abortions are performed every year;

- the consequence of these actions is 175 million pregnancies annually, less (+/–) 42 million abortions = 133 million live births (UN estimates for 1995–2000);

- 13 million of those births (9.8 per cent) occur in the developed countries and 120 million (90.2 per cent) in the underdeveloped countries.

According to the WHO and others, a high proportion of those 175 million pregnancies are undesired by the women (or the couples) concerned. Thirty million of these accidents occur among the 300 million couples using some form of (unreliable) RI. As for the 120 million fertile couples using no RI at all, but who say they would if they could, let us estimate conservatively that one-third of them, some 40 million, will conceive. These two groups together would thus account for 70 million unwanted pregnancies or 40 per cent of all the pregnancies, desired or undesired, which occur annually.

Even using this conservative estimate and even assuming that all the present abortions are performed solely for the benefit of these two groups, satisfying the demand for RI on the part of 70 million couples would reduce pregnancies from 175 million at present to 105 million. Even if all those babies were born live, this would still represent 28 million fewer children than the 133 million born at present annually. In reality, the impact would be far greater. This calculation concerns only the two groups, using RI or not, who say they want to space or stop births. These 420 million represent only a fraction, some 35 per cent, of the Third World women between the ages of 15 and 49, who number about 1.2 billion. What if the other 780 million women could be reached with RI techniques during their fertile years?

If their birth rates were the same as those of women in the developed countries, all Third World women taken together would have 53 million babies a year instead of 120 million; the total annual number of births in the world would be 66.5 instead of 133 million! If annual deaths were increased by merely one-third, population would immediately begin to decline.

We do not expect miracles, but we do seek to point out the scope for substantial, not to say spectacular progress. How might such amelioration in RI be achieved?

Ways and Means

RI techniques are well known: abortion is one avenue; male and female sterilisation and contraception are the other.

Abortion

Although we have taken the figures immediately above at face value, we noted earlier with some scepticism the United Nations' claim that each year an average of 45 million abortions are performed. About 24 million of these operations are legal; the WHO terms the rest 'unsafe', which does not mean that in practice 'legal' equals 'safe'. Among the 'unsafe', 90 per cent take place in the Third World. At least 70,000 women die as a result, including 40,000 in Asia and 23,000 in Africa. Women understand the risks. For example, of the women hospitalised in Bolivia for abortion complications, only 7 per cent had ever used contraception but 77 per cent said they wanted to do so.[3]

In many places, particularly in the former communist countries of Eastern Europe, abortion is routinely practised as a form of contraception, to the point that there is one abortion for every live birth. In Latin America, the ratio is said to be one in two or three. India officially counted 4.3 million abortions in 1990 while China reported zero ... We recognise the obstacles to accurate tallies; even so, the UN's world figures strike us as either too high (total number of abortions) or too low (total deaths).

Be that as it may, assuming the figures are accurate, they underscore the utter wastefulness of abortion as a Population Reduction Strategy or as a Reproductive Inhibitor, even if they do, supposedly, prevent 45 million births a year. Whether 'safe' or 'unsafe', abortions are for our purposes an insignificant cause of female mortality, and are costly in financial terms, in time lost and in medical complications, to women, to families and to nations.

For the price –in the broad sense – of 45 million abortions, genuine RI contraceptive and sterilisation services could be provided to huge numbers of men and women. Abortion is not just economically wasteful but physiologically inefficient since another pregnancy can occur as soon as menstruation returns. It should remain an option, and be legalised wherever this is not the case, but it should certainly be downgraded as a strategic option and not relied upon as a genuine PRS.

Sterilisation

We recommend enlisting the stridently militant US anti-abortion forces to finance and possibly even participate in Third World sterilisation campaigns. This would satisfy their own avowed objectives since sterilisation is an absolute guarantee against abortion and could significantly reduce the number of these legal or illegal operations worldwide. At the moment, China and India lead the world in numbers of sterilisations although the technique is gaining some importance in other countries like Mexico.

Peru's programme could also serve as a model. Mobile health squads are present on village market days, they attract women with banners and bands, offer them gifts of clothing, shoes and foodstuffs in exchange for a free, painless tubal ligation which takes only ten minutes. One hundred thousand such operations are now performed yearly, as well as 10,000 vasectomies. Some Peruvian parliamentarians and women's groups have protested that the sterilised women, many of them poor Indians, are illiterate and do not understand what they are signing for, but the Health Ministry can point to great successes in family planning, claiming that in addition to the sterilisations, millions of pills and condoms distributed free have allowed 900,000 couples to avoid unwanted pregnancy. Dispensaries and individual health workers have incentives to meet RI targets since their jobs may depend on it. They receive bonuses for exceeding sterilisation quotas.

Neighbouring Brazil, on the other hand, has its policies back to front. It does not allow female sterilisation at all unless it is discovered to be necessary 'during another operative procedure'. The result is thousands of unnecessary Caesarean births. One-third of all deliveries in Brazil are Caesareans, a rate even higher than in the US where the obstetrician's convenience usually comes first. In Brazil, this is the only way that women can legally obtain sterilisation after childbirth.

Sweden had a sterilisation (eugenics) programme from 1934 to 1974 which carried out 62,000 operations over the four decades. When in 1997 a leading newspaper published an investigation of the programme, a great outcry ensued, but it had operated in full public view during those 40 years and was generally regarded as progressive. It held down welfare state expenditures by targeting people who received high benefits because of their physical degeneracy or anti-social behaviour. Similar eugenics programmes existed on a smaller scale in other Nordic countries, Switzerland and the USA.

Undoubtedly, some of these operations were abusive. One Swedish girl was thought irredeemably stupid and so was sterilised; in fact she could not read the blackboard at school and needed spectacles rather than a ligation. Statistically, however, these programmes did target the physically and mentally unfit. For PRS purposes, as we have repeatedly stressed, it is impossible to deal at all times with individuals. One must be content with statistically significant methods. In any case, a country like Sweden no longer needs a programme of this type, or possibly only a very small one.

We emphasise the humanitarian impact of sterilisation, since close to 600,000 women now die of abortions, pregnancy complications or in childbirth every year, the equivalent of four jumbo jet crashes a day. These deaths provide another demonstration of economic and physiological inefficiency (orphans left behind, overburdened hospitals, dead women's husbands continuing to impregnate others, and so on). The unfortunate women concerned would have been better off sterilised than dead.

The WHO insists that sterilisation, because it is permanent, must be 'free of inducements' in order to insure informed consent. For our part, we see a good case for attracting poor and prolific women with inducements and suggest, on the contrary, that the practice be generalised.

We underscore also the need for one-stop services like Peru's so that women can obtain sterilisation *with or without the consent of their husbands*. The question of confidentiality is crucial. Some studies show that up to one-half of all births are unwanted (by women) while men often equate power ('being a real man') with large numbers of offspring, especially sons. Men's lives are not endangered by multiple pregnancies and unsafe deliveries so they are never sanctioned for their macho attitudes. The mothers-in-law of millions of hapless women are another huge source of pressure to bear children.

Contraception

Such social pressures and the needs of poor women in populous countries should guide us in our assessments of contraception and of the means to achieve it which are presently on offer. One stark reality is that millions of women, especially poor ones, have little control over their own lives and their own bodies. Furthermore, for most of them, in their precarious situations, infertility would be the ultimate disaster. They could then easily be abandoned by their husbands with no resources and no prospects (except, perhaps, prostitution). Their own families would not take them back either. Failure to produce sons also provides frequent grounds for desertion. Let us look at some typical concrete problems faced by women in poor and populous countries.

- Chandra is Indian, 25 years old, the second wife of a fairly well-off man who left his first spouse to marry her. She has had three daughters; after the birth of the third one, the first wife ridiculed her for not being able to bear sons so Chandra became pregnant again right away. She haemorrhaged heavily during delivery but at least the fourth child was a boy. Chandra wanted to be sterilised but while she was still in hospital, her youngest daughter fell ill with malaria. She left hospital against medical advice to care for the child, who died in spite of her efforts. Chandra still wants to be sterilised, but what if her only son dies? She is afraid that she will become pregnant again and that she will die if she has another child. Her husband, she says, is 'very demanding'.

- Sadia is a rural Bangladeshi, 13 years old, and is engaged to be married to a man she has never met. She has just begun to menstruate and has already learned to observe certain taboos during her period to avoid heavy bleeding and painful cramps. She no longer goes to school and will soon be married. Like many village women she is sequestered at home but she doesn't mind because women who venture into the outside world alone become easy targets for censure, harassment and violence and may end up as prostitutes, with no protection from anyone.

- Tina is a Filipina, 20 years old and has a boyfriend she loves but they are too poor to get married. Like virtually everyone else in the Philippines, she is Catholic but like more than 1 million of other young, unmarried Filipinas, that doesn't prevent her from having sexual relations with her boyfriend. Unfortunately for Tina, a 1989 agreement between Church and state limits family planning services, such as they are, to married couples. Like 13–37 per cent of Filipina women she has undergone an illegal abortion. She is thankful that there were no complications and thinks she is lucky compared to her best friend who had to have an abortion after being raped. Rape in Metro Manila has risen by 18 per cent in the past decade.[4]

In order to practise contraception or to be sterilised, Third World women require three things presently in extremely short supply: knowledge, means and power. The Commissioning Parties surely cannot supply all three to all Third World women, but they can and should recognise that many current RI programmes are flawed on at least one of these counts, and more often than not, on all three.

Millions of women have little knowledge of their own reproductive systems and of the options available to control their fertility. Even when they have theoretical access to family planning means, services may be erratic and supplies irregular. As for power, it would be an especially brave woman who openly defied her husband's (or her mother-in-law's) authority. The set of obstacles to be overcome in the practice of RI is therefore formidable.

Assuming, however, that more time, effort, money and pressure are applied to solving the problems described, what would be the ideal contraceptive for the millions of women who do not want, or no longer want, or ought not to have children? The first thing to acknowledge is that this miracle RI technique does not exist.

In-depth, cross-cultural investigations covering thousands of Third World women show that if it did, it would be (1) long-acting (from five to seven years) but reversible; (2) would not produce side-effects noticeable either to the woman herself or to her sexual partner; (3) could be ingested, injected, inserted or implanted confidentially and (4) would be affordable and reliable.

- *Long-acting but reversible*: intra-uterine devices (IUDs) and Norplant best fit the description. IUDs work for ten years or longer; Norplant (slow hormone releaser rods which are implanted in the underarm) works for five, but both may provoke some side-effects.

- *Absence of side-effects*: women say that family planning services often ignore their complaints concerning side-effects and act as if they should just grin and bear them. *We wish to point out that whatever the method chosen, every unsatisfied 'customer' directly discourages a number of her female friends who will rightly or wrongly forgo contraception on the basis of her horror stories.* Conversely, every contented contraceptive user will encourage her gossip group to try it as well. Here is one area where we cannot afford to employ *only* the statistical method: individual satisfaction counts in the longer run.

  Injectable contraceptives like Depo-Provera only work for a month and often provoke heavy bleeding. They also may inadvertently transmit HIV unless the needles are changed or sterilised. Barrier methods (diaphragm, female condom) have the fewest side-effects, and in addition the female condom protects against AIDS, but they are not especially confidential and women may be culturally loath to insert anything into their own vaginas.

- *Confidential*: hormonal contraceptives (the pill) are reasonably confidential but many studies have shown that any method requiring constant, daily attention doesn't work, at least not on the necessary scale.

  Immuno-contraceptives would be ideal in respect to confidentiality and would work for six to twelve months, but their development is miserably funded and their generalisation as a genuine, widespread option is probably five to seven years away.

- *Affordable and reliable*: the cheapest and surest RI technique is also the oldest – *coitus interruptus* – but it is nobody's idea of a good time. Most other methods are 92–98 per cent sure. Affordability depends crucially on the governments involved which can make contraception and sterilisation free if they so choose. Pharmaceutical companies could also make a contribution. We suggest that the Commissioning Parties encourage them to do so.

Recommendations

Some years ago, fanciful scenarios involving the mixing of hormonal contraceptives with water or flour for mass distribution were bandied about. These plots are the purest science fiction. One could scarcely build a factory large enough to manufacture the requisite hormonal RI to put in wells; the active substance would degenerate in the food, and so on. Since externally imposed, mass RI is out of the question, it is imperative to start from *what women themselves want*. The problem then becomes one of supplying them with what they want in a form they can use. We cannot, however, leave everything to individual will and ignore the need for *statistically effective RI*. Norplant can be an effective tool for controlling fertility among irresponsible or socially undesirable groups.

Some states in the USA already require women convicted of drug abuse to have an implant. Incentives are provided to black teenagers or women on welfare to use it as well. From the state treasury's point of view, as proposed in Kansas, it is preferable to pay a woman $500 to use Norplant than pay $205,000 to raise a child at the state's expense. In the Third World, Indonesian soldiers have rounded up East Timorese women so that they could be forcibly implanted.

Also promising, although less long-acting, would be immuno-contraceptives, also known as 'anti-fertility vaccines', now under study and in some cases already the subject of clinical trials. We prefer the term 'immuno-contraceptives' since 'anti-fertility vaccine' is repellent to many women, equating fertility as it does with a communicable disease. The term could be misunderstood to mean *permanent* loss of fertility and could be used for propaganda purposes by anti-PRS activists. Whatever the name, the scientific principle remains the same: the woman's immune system is primed to react against impregnation and foetal implantation. The immune reaction can be either anti-sperm or anti-egg.

It will come as no surprise that the 'human rights' brigades with their individualistic approach are once more pitted against the longer-term health of the planet and that of Third World women themselves, most of whom deeply desire more efficient methods for controlling their fertility.

Critics claim that this innovative method, which should be seen as a possibly revolutionary tool for individual and human survival, furnishes 'an unprecedented potential for abuse' of individual users, apparently because immuno-contraceptives could be administered 'on a mass scale with or without a person's knowledge or consent because the delivery system will be an injection, pill or drinking liquid'.[5]

These immuno-contraceptives are not geared to work for more than six months to one year, although researchers hope eventually to extend the duration of effective protection to 12–18 months. Feminist activists appear to believe that women's 'capacity to choose' must be exercised on a day-to-day basis; that any method preventing pregnancy for a longer period is somehow abusive of female free will.

We see such alarmist and dogmatic reactions as mistaken, particularly given the huge unmet need *as expressed by women themselves*. The warm welcome they have given such long-term solutions as Norplant, IUDs and sterilisation shows that 'choice' is an elastic notion. One could counter the feminist premise that choice must be day to day by pointing out that these longer-term solutions *cannot be taken away from women*; at least they give them a little more power over their fertility in a context where abuse does not come from outside the home. The more RI methods that can be made available for women to choose from, the better.

Various studies have shown that non-prescription, over-the-counter sales and distribution of cheap oral contraceptives could help to generalise their use both in US inner cities and in the Third World where there are few doctors to prescribe and where at present only 38 million women rely on the pill. Cultural ways of ensuring reliable ingestion should also be explored. For example, in one large-scale trial in India, women were told to take the pill every night with a glass of milk. The women came back regularly for their 'milk pills' and refused to change for another contraceptive because 'this would deny them access to the only glass of milk their mothers-in-law were now obliged to give them daily.[6]

The best 'contraceptive' method of all would be mass female education, although we recognise that this is not a workable option under current circumstances. Proof has been administered time and again that fertility reduction is best served by more years in school for girls and ongoing education for women. The World Bank constantly repeats this mantra, but its own structural adjustment programmes militate against it. When the family cannot afford to educate all the children, the boys come first. For the moment, for better or for worse, the Peruvian incentives or the Norplant model remain the most viable options in a world where truly informed choice and control of one's own fertility are luxuries.

What About Men?

Men are notoriously touchy about anything relating to their sexuality and harbour irrational fears that vasectomy will harm their potency. The only other options open to males willing to take responsibility for contraception are the condom or withdrawal but in any event, most of them place the burden of RI entirely on women's shoulders (or, more accurately, reproductive organs). 'It was her risk and her decision', is one leitmotif. The other is described by Turkish doctors visiting couples at home to discuss family planning: 'Ignore her, she is like a chair. I decide what family planning we use', says the husband, refusing to let his wife speak.

The WHO is also developing a hormonal contraceptive for men which reduces sperm counts to undetectable levels. Limited trials involving 401 couples in nine countries have shown that the method is reliable and safe. All the babies born to couples after they stopped the treatment have been healthy and normal.

This method requires weekly injections – a serious drawback. The WHO is looking for longer-acting combinations and lower hormonal doses but this research, like much other RI work, is gravely underfunded. And if a male pill were developed, would women trust men to take it? Opinion surveys suggest that they might not.

We recommend much more generous financing for both medical and social science research on RI as well as for actual delivery programmes. Large numbers of RI paramedics need to be trained and given incentives to meet or exceed RI quotas. This recommendation applies to inner cities in the North as well as to Third World settings.

Numerous carrot-and-stick approaches could be put into practice immediately. National RI programmes could be greatly strengthened if they were part of structural adjustment conditionality. Countries being 'bailed out' by the IMF should be judged by their efficacy in reducing population growth rates and have their loans curtailed when targets are not met. Donors to refugee programmes should insist that women in camps be given incentives to be sterilised on site.

More generally, policies should be geared to rewarding women and couples for having one child or none (for instance, preference in hiring and promotion, places in school, access to housing, reduced prices for transport and essential items) and penalised for having many. At the moment, China wields the stick but not the carrot. A more rational approach for all countries would reduce the economic value of children and compensate in concrete, measurable terms families that limit their size.

2.5

Puzzles

Some areas of the global scene requiring a mention do not fit a convenient category or overlap many of them; they further present particular problems or ambiguities for PRS. We will comment briefly on three of them.

The Chinese Puzzle

One of the greatest obstacles to the overarching objective of population reduction can be summed up in a single word: China. One person in five on earth is Chinese. Whatever happens there is of immense concern to the rest of the world. If, in order to arrive at a global population of 4 billion in 2020, every country were to be assessed on a *pro rata* basis, China would have to reduce its numbers from 1.2 billion to 800 million. The magnitude of the task is staggering. Yet China must somehow submit to PRS.

This country occupies more of the globe's surface territory than any other country save Canada or Russia and is a highly structured state with traditions dating back 3,500 years. In spite of resounding political failures like the 'Great Leap Forward', at the end of the twentieth century it is less susceptible than most developing countries to the traditional 'Horsemen' scourges.

China is unlikely to succumb to the sirens of *war* in spite of a powerful professional army of over 3 million. Hong Kong has already come back into the motherland's fold without firing a shot and Macau will soon follow. China sees its occupation of Tibet as the 'recovery of a former possession'. Some potential exists for conflict with Taiwan which China still considers one of its provinces; possibly with Vietnam or the Philippines over the small, uninhabited Spratly islands in the South China Sea which it claims as part of its 'Sacred Territory'. More to the point, these islands have proven offshore oil reserves. There is no obvious civil or ethnic conflict inside mainland China. However, if

Taiwan escapes its grasp, China fears this might encourage Muslim and Buddhist regions to sue for independence.

Provocation and possible explosion is not impossible, but war of any kind holds little interest at present for the average Chinese. Incitement to conflict would need to be handled with enormous care, particularly because of the potential impact on Japan. Japan should be allowed to develop its full military potential. It is a vital stabilising power in Asia and may need to use force if competition for food and for local energy supplies to fuel continuing growth becomes more and more acute.[1]

Since China is now the world's largest cereals producer, *famine* of the sort that killed some 30 to 40 million people in the early 1960s is not a credible threat. China will still need increasingly to call on the West's food exports and for the West this could prove an important bargaining chip.

As for *pestilence*, China now harbours a quarter of the world's tuberculosis cases. It is using financial incentives to combat the disease, paying 'barefoot doctors' one dollar for every case they identify and $5 dollars for every patient who successfully completes the treatment. However, the high rate of TB infection will be a plus because AIDS has as yet scarcely been acknowledged and will spread before the government admits that there is a problem. To date, accurate figures concerning Chinese AIDS cases are unavailable but they are probably still in the low tens of thousands.

WHO officials say that Asia will surpass Africa in the number of HIV/TB deaths by the year 2000; one claims that 'there are millions and millions of people infected with TB in Asia just waiting for HIV to come along and activate it. It's a disaster waiting to happen.' We cannot say what the eventual incidence of HIV/TB will be in China, but the usual denial syndrome should allow it to take hold.

The biggest contributor we foresee to Chinese mortality will be none of the Horsemen but rather environmental collapse. As a population regulator, ecological damage is a double-edged sword. Some sources of pollution can be contained within the country's frontiers; others pose an increasing threat to the planet in its entirety. Reports of severe land, air and water pollution with deleterious health effects are trickling out of China. One excellent recent report by an eyewitness American journalist describes the devastating ecological costs of rapid industrialisation.[2]

The automobile transport option, acid rain, leaded petrol, unwashed coal, soil erosion, deforestation, toxic wastes, fouled rivers – the list goes on. However, until the level of poison reaches true crisis proportions, the government is unwilling to act since it knows that any improvement in the environment will be immediately paid for in job losses and ensuing social strife.

Only when thousands of people dependent on the Huai river for drinking water fell ill did the government finally decide to act, closing down paper mills and factories which had been emptying untreated wastes for years directly into the river. When the situation is merely flirting with crisis, the governmental attitude remains, 'Heavy pollution may kill you in a hundred days but without heat and food you die in three.'

According to the same reporter, ordinary Chinese, even well-educated ones, actually believe that one can develop 'tolerance' or immunity to foul air and they are quite prepared to pay the ecological price for industrial development guaranteeing their own financial enrichment. Already one-quarter of deaths in China result from respiratory ailments. The impact of heavy pollution is compounded by the tobacco epidemic.

The degradation of the environment can only spread as the country seeks to meet its voracious energy needs by burning low-grade, sulphurous coal. China intends to triple its 1991 power generation capacity of 150 gW to 430 gW in 2010 and to double car ownership in the next few years. This is CO_2, climate-altering pollution which will affect plenty of people besides the Chinese.

What is the Chinese population? Officially, 1.2 billion; in fact no one knows. China instituted its so-called 'one-child policy' in 1979 and has perpetuated the illusion in the outside world that the policy is actually being enforced. This is far from the case, particularly in the rural areas. Government bureaucrats may have to follow the rules because they can be easily punished but tens of millions of peasant families pay scant attention to government decrees: 'The mountains are high and the Emperor is far away.' Party officials also have a deep career interest in reporting low birth rates in their district ...

The combination of frightening pollution and out-of-hand population growth could paradoxically be the key to solving the Chinese puzzle. If the programme were properly presented as being in China's own best interests, China could conceivably be brought to *cooperate* actively in PRS. The danger is that it might seem to be a scheme hatched by the West in order to weaken China, an impression which must be avoided at all costs.

Chinese officials already recognise the danger of huge labour surpluses. Estimated in the mid-1990s at 150 million, the number of jobless rural people is likely to reach 370 million in the year 2000 and perhaps 450 million by 2010, according to state sources. Migration pressures on towns and cities could become overwhelming. Rural industries absorbed only 5.3 million people from 1988 to 1994 and cannot possibly deal with the oncoming tide, particularly since the government has finally elected to practise 'survival of the fittest' policies with regard to bloated and inefficient state industries.

Its aim is to reduce the present 130,000 publicly owned enterprises to 512 large, strategic conglomerates which will be opened up to foreign capital. Foreigners have already invested $64 billion. The government says that at least one-third of its present state companies are losing money. Trying to support this artificial economy is, to use a vivid Chinese expression, 'as impossible as ten fingers trying to hold down hundreds of fleas'.

As globalisation takes hold and the same winner/loser, In/Out rules apply in China as elsewhere, millions of Chinese 'fleas' will find themselves jobless. The government claimed 688 million total employment in 1996 but this figure masks a decade's decline in stable employment and a sharp increase in contract and temporary work. Millions of lay-offs are occurring in textiles, railways and heavy industry. The Harbin region north-east of Beijing, formerly the industrial heartland, is fast turning into a rust belt, an evolution familiar in the USA and Great Britain. Many redundant workers receive no benefits at all.

Foreign companies employ directly very few people, preferring to subcontract. For example, Nike has been much criticised for its labour policies but actually owns no factories at all in China. Ultimately, the Chinese will blame their government for decreasing numbers of jobs and increasingly appalling working conditions for those who have them.[3]

The Chinese hold out the vague hope that the unemployed millions will somehow find salvation in the 'service economy'. Some of them may; most will become vagrants. It is this surplus, unabsorbable population that defines the area for cooperation with the West. The rich world can provide technical expertise and finance for solving problems of mutual concern, not least the reduction in the huge numbers of Chinese. Otherwise we, and the world's climate, will pay.

What if China were to refuse to cooperate? If nothing is done, its population is officially slated to reach 1.4 billion Chinese in 2010 and 1.7 billion in 2025. These are minimum estimates, based on a present population of 1.2 billion which may well be seriously understated. Whatever the real figure, this pressure will intensify all China's current problems. The environment will suffer one indignity after another, implying eventual local if not national collapse, particularly as regards water (to be noted in more detail below). By 2010, the government will have to provide well over 500 million tonnes of food and feed grains to people who have become accustomed to better diets.

As its capacity to restore ecological balance and maintain nutritional adequacy becomes problematic at best, China can either join in PRS strategies on a crash basis, or seek *Lebensraum*. We assume that Western military specialists are fully cognisant of the dangers of Chinese expansionism on grounds of gross overpopulation, resource shortages and ecological abuse.

We urge that China's leadership be made fully aware of the inadvisability and eventual military consequences of the second option. China, rather, has every interest, including that of state survival, in cooperating in PRS. Encouraging and aiding the Chinese to understand this reality should be a top diplomatic priority.

The Water Puzzle

China also takes pride of place when we examine the world's most indispensable resource. We have already considered some questions relating to water in our discussions of food supplies and disease but we have not done justice to its full strategic importance. Not for nothing has water been labelled 'blue gold'. It will be among the most precious commodities on offer in many countries. Imagine a substance at once indispensable, without any possible substitutes and increasingly scarce: this is a scenario for remarkable profits but also for conflict.

Water is unequally distributed between countries and within them and in many places drinking water is already in extremely short supply. According to the World Bank, 80 countries with 40 per cent of the world's population are suffering from water scarcity whereas just nine countries have 60 per cent of all the fresh water resources.

Not only must rural African women walk untold miles to fetch water but their urban counterparts must queue for water that is often unfit to drink. Alternatives are to pirate it from water mains or purchase it from cistern trucks. In addition to food access, access to water is becoming a severely limiting factor of human existence even though no UN agency has yet defined 'water security'.

Chinese city dwellers are a case in point. In Beijing, one-third of the wells have already run dry due to over-pumping for outlying wheat and millet production. The water table has dropped to 50 metres below sea level and is causing serious subsidence problems. It continues to be drawn down at the rate of a metre or two a year, to the point that China's capital city might have to be transferred elsewhere. China's water minister has himself recognised publicly that half of China's 600 large- and medium-sized cities face water shortages; over 100 are classed as seriously deprived.

The situation is not helped by the thousands of Chinese factories which are spewing toxic chemicals into rivers that people depend on for agriculture and for their drinking water. Two-thirds of the Chinese drinking water supply does not meet World Health Organisation minimum standards.

When we look at water use, we find some of the same Malthusian factors that we discovered with regard to food: since 1940, population has nearly tripled, but water consumption has quadrupled. Nuclear fusion or other cheap energy technology for desalination of seawater is not going to arrive in time to prevent serious shortages. The only new source of water is to stop wasting it, which means that it has to be professionally managed, preferably by a private company, and priced according to real costs of maintenance and delivery.

When transnational companies move into a city like Buenos Aires or Casablanca, service improves and waste is eliminated. Such services must be paid for. If slum neighbourhoods cannot afford to be connected to the watermains and pay for the service, they should be bypassed. With 50 per cent of the world's population already living in cities, we know that demand for fresh water cannot be met. It must therefore be rationed in the only way feasible: by price. Some will have to make do with untreated water as 1.4 billion people are already said to do. The return of cholera to Latin America is, for example, directly linked to urban growth and insufficient supplies of fresh water.

A strategic analysis of available supplies reveals that the future will be rife with water wars. Of the world's 200 largest river systems, 150 are shared by two nations, and the other 50 are shared by three to ten nations. For example, eight upstream countries can take water from the Nile before it reaches Egypt, yet Egypt depends on the Nile for almost its entire water supply. Many other similar situations exist and one immediately sees the potential for fomenting conflict.

Although it is beyond the scope of our own study, we recommend drawing up a 'water flashpoints' map which would include physical, political and strategic data. Such a map would highlight areas where war, famine and pestilence will be able to give their full measure.

The Drug Puzzle

The consensus of the Working Party is that all drugs, 'hard' and 'soft', should be legalised. We recognise that in most Western countries it is difficult to campaign on such a platform and that the issue of decriminalisation neither pleases nor attracts politicians. It is also quite possible that precious time and energy would be squandered on the battle for substance legalisation at a time when Western powers should be directing their efforts towards selective PRS at home and abroad. Thus we cannot say peremptorily that the Commissioning Parties should champion such a cause.

Nonetheless we favour legalisation for several compelling reasons. At the most conservative estimate, drug-related activities represent at least 2 per cent of gross world product, with some sources placing the value of the traffic two to three times higher. Even at the lower end of the scale, the least one can say is that narcotics are the most profitable commodity in the world. The turnover in illegal drugs represents 10 to 13 per cent of the value of world trade, more than all petroleum products combined. If the drug business were a national economy, it would be about number ten in the world, larger, for example, than that of Canada.

We see no reason why such revenues should continue to enrich the international criminal class and the most despicable elements of Western societies. It would be far preferable to hold this trade up to the light and subject it to legal and fiscal audit like any other business. Pharmaceutical, agribusiness or even entertainment-media corporations would be well placed to take on the production and marketing of legalised drugs and could be held accountable for the purity and quality of their merchandise.

This is considerably more than one can say for the present purveyors. Because they are forbidden, drugs are not only of dubious quality but are excessively expensive. Revenues are pumped into other criminal enterprises and sustain the money launderers who have given legitimate finance a bad name. As for the corrupting influence of drugs on government at every level, years of unsavoury revelations concerning at least a dozen countries suggest that further documentation is no longer required on that score.

Anyone arguing for the decriminalisation of drugs must inevitably make the comparison with Prohibition in America. Since Repeal, the population of the United States has not become noticeably more alcoholic. Even if it had, we believe that any adult should be free to decide if he or she wishes to drink, or take drugs, or for that matter smoke cigarettes or commit suicide.

Particularly in the United States, the drug trade has fatefully overloaded the prisons and the court system. Three per cent of the adult male black population is behind bars, mostly for drug offences. In addition to 1.8 million people (of all colours) in prison, a further 2.3 million have criminal records and are out on probation and parole. Conservative estimates from the US Office of National Drug Control Policy confirm that the

American economy suffers losses of at least $146 billion yearly because of drugs, including the social costs of drug-related crime calculated at $67 billion.

Since the outset of the Reagan administration, the US has declared a 'war on drugs'. The programme may be a crowd-pleaser politically but were it a real war, it would be considered a worse defeat than Vietnam. This is not for want of trying.[4]

The results of international participation (the UN, the G-7, the Council of Europe, the EC, and so on) in the 'war' are equally disappointing. Interpol spends half its budget on combating the drug trade. Despite all these efforts, only an estimated 10 per cent of drugs produced worldwide are seized by the authorities. Because the rewards are high, many people are willing to take tremendous risks to transport and market drugs.

Europe has not taken a position on drug legalisation either, thereby strengthening various local Mafias and foreign militaries. Source countries, for which drugs are indirectly big money-earners, cooperate with their Northern counterparts only when absolutely forced or blackmailed and there is no reason why they should behave differently in future. If drugs were legalised, source countries could allow cultivation, processing and export and earn tax revenues on these activities. There would be no more spraying of smallholders' farms and other physical destruction of resources.

Each passing year confirms that police and armies cannot interdict supplies. Even so, the United States government intends to spend another $16 billion in drug war efforts in 1998, for interception at its borders, eradication in source countries plus a small amount for 'drug education' at home. Large sums will once more be channelled to corrupt Latin American military establishments which will proceed to use their counter-insurgency equipment against their own political enemies rather than against the drug kingpins. Their priorities are rarely the same as those of the US anti-drug warriors. It would be more efficient to devote such princely sums to preventive and curative PRS.

US armed forces are no match for the drug barons either. As one US military official wrote, 'Just as in Vietnam, the overwhelming advantages the United States possesses in technology, intelligence services and military strength are not sufficient to overcome the political, economic and social factors that influence the drug war ... [However, it is] easier from a political standpoint to plunge ahead rather than conduct a serious reassessment.'[5]

We recommend that such a serious reassessment be undertaken without delay and that it calculate the advantages of legalising drugs to the world economy. At present, they are far too costly in economic, social, military and political terms and divert scarce resources from areas where they would do more good.

Were legal companies to sell legal drugs, they should not be held responsible for individual abuse but, like the tobacco industry, they should be obliged to provide warnings. Clear labelling of contents as 'addictive' (where valid) or as 'dangerous to health' would be required. For younger people, the same legal age limits could be applied to drugs as to alcohol and driving under the influence subject to the same penalties. This is one area where governments might need to apply price controls or sell to some users in designated shops if prices tended to encourage black markets and crime as they do in the illegal drug economy.

Drugs should not be glamourised but if people want to kill themselves with overdoses, they should be allowed to get on with it. Considering the sorts of people who have done this so far, they would be doing society a signal service. From a PRS viewpoint, the mortality rates are negligible and would probably remain stable or drop slightly. An estimated 20,000 deaths occur annually from drug-related causes in the United States (1986–96). Figures for other countries are unreliable or unavailable, with only 11,000 deaths worldwide reported to the WHO, clearly an understatement. Drugs are a 'puzzle' area requiring more study but they have a major economic and minor PRS potential.

In Fine ...

This Report has attempted to provide the Commissioning Parties with a clear and responsible assessment of the situation faced by global capitalism and the market economy in the twenty-first century (Part One) and with the theoretical and practical means for avoiding potential disaster and paralysis (Part Two).

Although we will be gratified if this text is found timely, we do not consider ourselves as part of the millennial deluge, nor our Report a contribution to its documentary flood. We would have written essentially the same text five or ten years ago, five or ten years' hence. A few figures and references would be changed, but the message would not.

We have ourselves been altered by the experience of working together on this Report; our individual perceptions have coalesced and our awareness has been heightened. Urgency is now our paramount concern, one which it is difficult to evoke without recourse to the emotional language we have attempted to avoid in the Report itself.

We hope in particular that our factual method and detached approach have not obscured the need for political will and prompt action which can, perhaps, come only from an appeal both to reason and to emotion, first among them fear.

The Commissioning Parties, we surmise, have attained the stature that gave rise to the commissioning of this Report in the first place precisely because they do not fear to look reality in the face, because they understand the Roman wisdom *Necessitas non habet legem*, necessity knows no law.

We who have been privileged to contribute to this Report must now trust that their power to act is commensurate with their clairvoyance.

Annexe

Susan George

There are three ways of looking at this Report. The first is rejection: 'The Lugano Working Party's Worldwide Final Solution is too awful to be contemplated, therefore I shall not contemplate it.' Those who react in this way may wish to dispute the finer points of ostrich logic with other ostriches; I leave them to it and can do nothing further for them.

The second is to ask not whether the Working Party's choice is appalling – this much strikes me as obvious – but whether it is logically necessary. Once their premises were accepted, could their conclusions have been any different?

The third is to recognise that the conclusions do indeed follow from the premises and then to question the premises radically. These are of several kinds.

Premises

The *economic premises* are clear. Capitalist growth and efficiency are primary; all other values must be sacrificed to them. Competition in the marketplace (for jobs, for market share, for profits *inter alia*) will result in optimum efficiency because the market is the best allocator of all resources, whether natural, manufactured, financial or human. Markets are further capable of self-regulation and should not be interfered with.

The goals of economic activity are profit and accumulation which are both the sign and the measure of efficiency. Through financial markets, profits will be transformed into investment, allowing the whole cycle to begin again. Employment and the satisfaction of human needs, as opposed to those of the market itself, are incidental to the system which obeys the logic of supply and demand, not that of want and fulfilment.

A more or less fair distribution of assets between people in different parts of the world or between citizens of the same country may be the proper concern of governments or of charitable agencies; it is certainly not that of markets. Still, self-regulated markets are in a sense moral; they end up rewarding the hard-working, the serious and the 'deserving', or so their defenders claim. The system reserves its top prizes for radical, risk-taking individualism and, in this world, you're on your own.

This economic philosophy is championed especially by the very large transnational corporations or TNCs in manufacturing, services or finance which themselves attempt to reduce the pressures of competition, practising instead 'alliance capitalism'. Small- and medium-sized businesses, family firms, professionals, artisans, shop-owners do not generally function according to the same impersonal and remorseless rules. The true focus of the Report – because it is also the focus of the globalised market economy – is the freedom and welfare of the TNCs.

The social consequences deriving from the economic principles governing these corporations are plain. As the celebrated 'downsizer', Mr Albert ('Chainsaw Al') Dunlap, makes excruciatingly clear in his self-serving book, *Mean Business: How I Saved Bad Companies and Made Good Companies Great*,[1] corporations belong exclusively to those who invest in them, that is, to their shareholders.

They do not, conversely, belong to their employees, their suppliers or the communities in which they happen to be located. It follows that the corporate chief executive officer (CEO) must make as much money for his shareholders (and for himself) as he possibly can, by whatever means necessary. What happens to the people downsized, their families and the towns they live in is neither his concern nor his responsibility. End of story.

Downsizers like Mr Dunlap[2] are adulated by Wall Street and the City, enjoy huge compensation for their services and appear on magazine covers, although *Newsweek* once broke shockingly with tradition when it exposed several particularly brutal downsizing CEOs under the large red headline 'Corporate Killers'. *Newsweek* used figurative language; that of the Working Party is literal.

The average CEO of a major US corporation is now 'worth' an annual salary 200 to 300 times that of his lowliest employee. Meanwhile, wages for both British and American workers are lower in real terms than they were in 1987. For over a decade and a half, the rewards of increased productivity have left labour out. Workers everywhere are becoming more productive but are mostly penalised for their pains because globalisation pits them against each other in an international competitive war in which, to use Hobbes's words, 'Every man is enemy to every man.' The rewards flow towards top management and towards stockholders, that is, towards the owners of knowledge and of capital.

These companies are mobile and are the first to seek out new locations where unions are weak or outlawed and where they can find the highest possible productivity at the lowest possible wage. This phenomenon is not confined to the rich countries. The French TNC Thomson recently left Malaysia for Vietnam, leaving 2600 Malaysian workers behind. Nike has moved its subcontracting ('outsourcing') operations from the US to Korea to Indonesia to Vietnam, always on the lookout for a better deal.

Some scholars have gone to great lengths to demonstrate that downsizing and 'delocalisation' (moving from Flint, Michigan, to Shenzhen) are not the reason, or only a small part of the reason, for huge numbers of working poor in the US and for economic insecurity and mass unemployment in Europe. In any case, say these experts with exemplary and sudden concern for the downtrodden, Asians, Mexicans or Poles have just as much right to those jobs as we do. They imply or say outright that Americans and Europeans who want decent jobs at decent pay are being selfish towards the poor of the Third World.

The point is, rather, that transnationals are never going to solve *anyone's* employment problems. Compared to their size and sales, they supply precious few jobs. Although the UN says there are now about 40,000 TNCs, the top 100 of them control one-fifth of all TNC global assets. In 1996, these 100 stars sold over \$4.1 trillion worth of goods and services but employed fewer than 12 million people worldwide, less than the number they had on their payrolls in 1980! Between 1993 and 1996, they increased their sales by 24 per cent yet still managed to reduce their workforce. Every employee of one of the top TNCs, from the chairman to the janitor, now produces an average \$350,000 worth of sales. Now *that's* productivity.

The *political premises* of *The Lugano Report* derive from the economic ones. Social and political arrangements arrived at through the operation of markets, massive privatisation, reduction of state services and other neo-liberal measures are the best that have been or can be devised. As the Working Party puts it, 'The market, at its broadest and most inclusive, is the closest we are likely to come to the wisdom of the Almighty.' Even though it causes suffering for some and seems cruel when viewed superficially, it can still draw good out of apparent evil.

This is a familiar theme: capitalism cannot be improved upon and is the natural condition of mankind. The free market is a precondition for democracy, democracy is a precondition for stability and peace which in turn are preconditions for the continuation of business. In any event, thanks to the information technology revolution and the mobility of money, globalisation and market integration are inevitable and irresistible. It's like the old and terminally unfunny joke about rape: the only thing to do is lie back and enjoy it.

The globalised market should thus determine well-nigh all relations between individuals and societies. Since states can't do much about society, and shouldn't even if they could, democracy is not as important as it once was. It may supply a decorative façade, but democracy has to be kept under control (or phased out) because elections and mass participation by definition favour the masses, who are by definition losers. Lots of people loudly expressing themselves are likely to be irresponsible and can only get in the way.

As for *trade premises*, the Working Party favours unrestricted trade and investment with a strong 'rules-based' international legal framework to guarantee this freedom, like that of the World Trade Organisation. This is understandable from the TNCs' point of view because the world trade order is tailor-made for them. Their propaganda has been so effective that coming out against 'free trade' is now rather like coming out against motherhood. What lies behind the semantics?

Fully one-third of all world trade now consists of exchanges *within* the same firm; that is, Shell 'trading' with Shell, IBM with IBM, Unilever with Unilever. A further third of world trade is not intra-firm but inter-firm, or TNCs trading with each other – General Electric with General Motors. Only the remaining third of exchanges on world markets can in any normal sense be called 'national' trade and this share is steadily shrinking.

What Original Sin and the Holy Trinity are to Catholics, the benefits of free trade are to neo-liberals. This basic doctrine is founded on the rock of 'comparative advantage'. According to this well-known principle elaborated in the nineteenth century by David Ricardo, a country should sell what it produces relatively cheaply and buy what it produces relatively dearly. So far so good.

This theory presupposes, however, that, as in Ricardo's day, capital stays home and transport is costly, which the first no longer does and the second no longer is. It further assumes that commerce takes place *between nations* and completely leaves out the reality that TNCs can invest and produce anywhere; that their intra-firm and inter-firm exchanges already constitute two-thirds of world trade in goods and services.

In the more technical language of specialists, the 200-year-old theory which is still going strong calls on 'a simple two-country general equilibrium framework' which can only distort judgements about the benefits or disadvantages of denationalised, multi-polar TNC trade.[3]

But it is not just economic theory that is muddled and inadequate to deal with present empirical reality. Comparative advantage has always been concerned with the *economic* costs of producing wine and cloth, to use Ricardo's original illustration, in this or that country. We now live in a world where the norms and rules of the political and social systems of different countries are placed in direct competition.

Would you accept child labour, twelve-hour days, miserable wages, dangerous working conditions and bans on unions at home? Probably not. But if you see no reason why your compatriots should have to compete with the unfortunate and oppressed citizens of nations where all these practices are 'legal', then you are labelled 'anti-free trade', a 'protectionist', anathema.

The World Trade Organisation exempts goods made by prison labour from its rules but has nothing to say about the right to organise, working conditions or child labour. The International Textile, Garment and Leather Workers' Federation estimates that 250 million children are at work in the world, half of them under 14 years old, nearly all in outrageous conditions. This horror has nothing to do with culture, tradition or

'Asian values' but with getting three compliant and defenceless children for the price of one adult.

The federation says that these working children could all be put in school at a cost of $6 billion, or 2 per cent of the world armaments expenditure. The same arguments in favour of child labour have been trotted out for over a century, first in Britain and Europe, now in Pakistan or Honduras and by much the same sorts of people. Using children is the only way to keep the country's industry competitive; the kids will be even worse off, they'll starve or become prostitutes if they don't work for us; their families depend on them. The latest twist is the call for 'children's rights', including the 'right to work', such that school should not be compulsory at all.

Child labour in fact drives down wages and replaces adults. In India, the numbers of working children and jobless adults are roughly the same. The practice perpetuates poverty. Today's working children, if they aren't already dead, will be tomorrow's unemployed grown-ups, sending their own children out to work in the same sordid conditions. Plenty of TNCs are 'outsourcing' contracts to companies using children.[4]

Child labour also exists, albeit on a much smaller scale, in the North, but at least legislation in advanced countries recognises that contracting parties do not necessarily have equal bargaining power and that the weaker party must be afforded legal protection. Like the child, the worker is not always 'free' to exercise normal 'rights' and without such protection, the 'right to work' may mean accepting inhuman conditions in order to survive.

Thus a famous decision of the United States Supreme Court upholding a minimum wage law for women referred to their relative bargaining weakness which could make them the 'ready victims of those who would take advantage of their necessitous circumstances'.[5] It may come as a surprise to the Supreme Court, but globalisation and free trade are overruling its decision. This is why critics speak of 'the race to the bottom' when national standards are placed in competition with each other. The lowest common denominator tends to become the norm and for the individual, it comes down to a choice between Third World conditions and no job at all.

The same arguments can be applied to environmental standards except that nature has no bargaining power at all unless it is to buckle when it can no longer stand the assault. In the international trade regime, if a country can offer its products at a cheaper price because it practises political repression, closes it eyes to social oppression and rapes its environment, this is neither the neo-liberal economist's nor the World Trade Organisation's' problem.

The WTO suggests that grievances be addressed to the International Labour Organisation; mainstream economists say, 'Don't use trade to deal with humanitarian problems: let the losers migrate or send them massive technical and financial aid.' Fat chance. The present reality is that by the time a product reaches the market, it has lost all memory of human or natural abuse.[6]

The *financial premises* of the Report are simple. Capital is mobile (while labour is not). Financial markets theoretically allow those with savings to invest in stocks, bonds, options and so on in order to channel investment back into production and create welfare for all. In reality, only a tiny percentage of the huge flows of cash to financial markets is actually invested in the 'real' economy.[7]

The immense influx of liquid funds to financial markets also reflects the transfer of wealth from bottom to top. When less affluent people have a bit of cash in hand, they buy goods and services and keep the real economy ticking over. When money moves to those who already have much of what they need or want, it goes into largely unproductive paper. The Working Party scarcely considers the possibility that finance capital might be largely unrelated to the actual production and distribution of goods and services, although it is rightly fearful of volatility and crash.

The cash sloshing about the world is largely in the hands of pension funds, insurance companies and financial houses (brokerages, hedge-funds and the like). Their combined assets come to a tidy $21,000 billion, half of which belongs to US sources. This figure, which comes from the 1998 Report of the Bank for International Settlements (BIS), the Central Bankers' Central Bank, is incomprehensible to ordinary mortals. To put it in perspective, it amounts to more than the combined annual GNP of all the industrialised countries, or $3,500 for every man, woman and child alive today on the planet.

The managers of these colossal sums are constantly taking the temperature of the market and, when they move, they move fast and in droves. Thus the BIS does not hesitate to speak of 'herding' behaviour, as all the fund managers try to follow their most successful peers, those who have historically outperformed the market. A change of a mere 1 per cent in their portofolios is equal to one-quarter of the capitalisation of all the stock markets in "emerging" Asia, two-thirds of all the stockmarkets in Latin America. So it is not surprising that these markets experience rapid collapse when the herd bolts for the gate.

Many of these funds can themselves shrivel and cause disastrous domino effects because they are so highly leveraged – meaning that they borrow for speculative purposes dozens of times their actual capital base, using one loan as collateral for the next. International funds are unregulated and allowed to do as they please – then people are surprised when they do just that.

The *ecological premises* of *The Lugano Report* are accurate. It is rare that environmental reality enters the mindset of the neo-liberal economic diagnosis. The Working Party is correct in saying that immediate action is required – although not their sort of action.

The Report neglects, however, an important political-ecological aspect. Thirty years ago in a famous article cited by the Working Party, biologist Garrett Hardin posited 'The Tragedy of the Commons'.[8] Hardin assumed a group of pastoralists in which each 'rational herdsman' would try to take advantage of all the others by increasing his herd by one animal, then another, then another – until all the herdsmen were doing the same and the resource base – the pasture – collapsed.

Hardin is doubtless a competent biologist but he knows little about history and anthropology or observed human behaviour. Dozens of historical and contemporary examples – from medieval grazing lands to Maine lobster fisheries – demonstrate that common property is not over-exploited *so long as group members retain the power to define who is a member of the group and to manage their resources according to their own rules.*

Hardin assumes that capitalist values and individualistic, self-maximising behaviour always prevails in all societies at all times – an utterly false assumption, as Karl Polanyi and numerous anthropologists have demonstrated. The real problem is that people's resources and their power to manage them are being confiscated. That people might somehow have managed to survive and to sustain their resource base for centuries without the intervention of the World Bank or the TNCs is not a thought easily entertained by the Working Party.

As for the *demographic premises*, the notion of 'population' in the Report is subjective, treated as an absolute and as absolutely excessive. Yet the concept of population is always relative to the needs of a particular economic and political system. When discussing 'overpopulation', the obvious question is ' "over" in relation to whom and to what?' In the Report, this question is not asked because it has already been answered. Population is considered only in relation to the needs of the neo-liberal scheme of things, including its diminishing requirements for workers and its desire to retain all the other features of the system whatever the human costs.

The Fast Castes

Social disparities in a given society were once defined by relative bargaining power and the negotiating table was geographically grounded. People had to negotiate because they were going to have to go on living with each other in pretty much the same space. The new keywords are speed and mobility.

At the top of the global pyramid are the 'fast people', the owners of capital and skilled professionals whom Jacques Attali calls 'elite nomads' because they are in demand across borders, can go where they please and are always on the move. Below them is the vast pool of stationary, 'slow people' whose chief common characteristic is their substitutability, whether the substitution takes place North–North, North–South or South–South.

At least the Working Party gives a straightforward answer to the great question that others always seek to avoid and never mention in public: 'What are we going to do with the losers?' The Commissioning Parties of *The Lugano Report* are surely not foreign to the world of corporate power which does indeed have a problem with 'losers', particularly since they have themselves done so much to create them.

Defenders of the neo-liberal order affirm that it will eventually generate far more winners than losers because economic growth will one day provide enough for all and include everyone in its bounties. We shall all be beneficiaries. This claim constantly appears in the literature, from the International Monetary Fund to the International Chamber of Commerce, and serves as a justification for harsh policies, lay-offs and general human suffering which will be put right in some radiant future.[9]

The claim is a lie. Twenty-first-century politics will not be about pie-sharing, as it has been in the post-Second World War welfare state era, or about who gets what resources, when and how; it will not even be about who can give orders to whom. Politics will hinge on the deadly serious business of staying alive. This is the bottom line of the Report.

If there is still such a thing as the class struggle – and I believe there must be because the survival stakes are so high – it will take place this time between the fast and the slow, the mobile and the stationary, the rooted and the migratory. Elite nomads are by definition better positioned to win it; the question for them is how.

The Report's formula recognises the problem and the stakes; it looks for a foolproof way to ensure that the nomads can continue to move smoothly from one oasis to another, increase their herds of corporate camels, exchange their carpets and dates without hindrance while still preserving the desert ecology and preventing restlessness among the remaining natives.

However repellent their solution, the authors of *The Lugano Report* at least have the decency, which the IMF and similar agencies do not, to recognise that you can't have your cake and eat it; you can't have a global economy which enriches a few beyond any historical parallel, which pushes wealth inexorably upwards and creates losers by the tens of millions – all that and a pristine environment and a clean conscience besides.

As the Working Party also makes clear, dispensability is moving up the social scale. It's not just the Brazilian Indians, the American poor and other remote tribes. You, your family, your profession, your small- or medium-sized firm, your community, your natural habitat are coming into its sights. If transnational business has no responsibilities except to the owners of capital, if governments can't tax vanishing, mobile money and help millions of stationary people to survive, then the excess numbers of those people must be somehow eliminated, or ...

Alternatives

This section has to start on a personal note because frankly, power relations being what they are, I feel at once moralistic and silly proposing alternatives. More times than I care to count I have attended events ending with a rousing declaration about what 'should' or 'must' occur. So many well-meaning efforts so totally neglect the crucial dimension of power that I try to avoid them now unless I think I can introduce an element of realism that might otherwise be absent.

But one must also tread a fine line between realism and cynicism. The occasional partial victory showing that the mentality, the premises and the goals of the Working Party, its sponsors and others like them can be challenged and eventually vanquished because countless people are actually out there on the field doing good and necessary work of a thousand different kinds: this is what keeps me going.

However, because I am constantly being asked 'what to do', I begin with some negative suggestions. The first is not to be trapped by the 'should', the 'must' and the 'forehead-slapping school'. Assuming that any change, because it would contribute to justice, equity and peace, need only be explained to be adopted is the saddest and most irritating kind of naivety. Many good, otherwise intelligent people seem to believe that once powerful individuals and institutions have actually *understood* the gravity of the crisis (any crisis) and the urgent need for its remedy, they will smack their brows, admit they have been wrong all along and, in a flash of revelation, instantly redirect their behaviour by 180 degrees.

While ignorance and stupidity must be given their due, most things come out the way they do because the powerful want them to come out that way. I beg indulgence here for another personal story. In mid-1994, as an alleged expert on North–South issues, I was invited to speak at a UNESCO Colloquium on 'What

Happened to Development?' The Director-General was present as were various luminaries and official worthies of many nationalities who had, like me, been hovering around development debates for decades.

My turn came after many hand-wringing contributions on the proposed topic: no one could deny that there were more losers than ever before, that the top 20 per cent of humanity now controlled 84 per cent of the assets (as opposed to 70 per cent three decades earlier) while the bottom 20 per cent made do with a shade over 1 per cent of world wealth; that there were more malnourished, sick, jobless, hopeless people than ever, that 'development' was an abject failure.

I said I was embarrassed to be the only optimist in the hall. In my view development had been a tremendous success. Those who did not concur were perhaps using the wrong indicators and incorrect benchmarks to measure success and failure. I then proceeded to describe, giving chapter and verse, how debt and debt service had doubled in a decade, how dozens of countries were now subject to World Bank/IMF discipline and had been forcibly integrated into the global economy, how TNCs had found new freedom to invest and trade, how finance capital was rewarded as never before, how the powers of the state had been drastically curtailed and privatisation become the norm, how massive income transfers from poor to rich both within and between countries had become well entrenched.

If, I asked, the commercial banks, the official creditors, the Bank, the IMF, the TNCs, the money managers and the global elites were happy, who were we to complain? How could anyone affirm that development was *not* a success when everything had gone exactly to plan? Were not those who expected in addition fairer income distribution, an end to hunger, environmental renewal, universal education and health care being immoderately greedy?

The reader will be only mildly astonished to learn that I have not been asked back, but at least I didn't play stupid games. Everybody knows perfectly well what 'should' or 'must' be done if fairer income distribution, an end to hunger, and so on are really the goals. The problem is not to persuade those who stand in the way of these outcomes that their policies are mistaken but to get power. The problem is not to repeat mindlessly what 'should' or 'must' occur but to begin by asking two simple questions:

- Who is responsible for the present crisis?
- How can we make them stop?

Transnational Tyranny

Get power to do what? This question is more difficult than it might seem. I'm not happy with the ambiguity of the pronoun 'we', but I will use it here to encompass all those who reject *The Lugano Report* philosophy, are prepared to resist with whatever means they have at hand and are willing to fight for a different politics and a different world, not perfect but different.

In my view at least, the situation is fairly straightforward: 'we' have to find ways to stop people who will stop at nothing. Transnational capitalism can't stop. With TNCs and uninhibited financial flows it has reached a kind of malignant stage and will keep on devouring and eliminating human and natural resources even as it undermines the very body – the planet itself – upon which it depends.[10]

Codes of conduct and voluntary restraint are laughably (or weepingly) inadequate to protect nature and people from confiscation and destruction because their appropriation allows the cancer to spread for a while longer. This is why the stakes keep rising; this is also why I believe it is fruitless to ask TNCs to do a little less harm: we have to oppose what they *are*.

Faced with immensely powerful, non-transparent, completely unaccountable TNCs and the global governing structures they are putting in place to serve their interests; the burden 'we' must shoulder in the coming century is nothing less than the invention of international democracy. The alternative is totalitarianism and the Lugano solution; the choice is between their rules and ours.

We are in a similar position to that of the Americans or the French in the mid-eighteenth century. They too were groping, not entirely sure how to get out from under an absolutist monarchy and move to a national democracy; to change their status from subjects to citizens. They didn't have a perfect blueprint (no one ever has) and finally they had to fight.

I don't know if our century is more mature, if we can invent non-violent solutions and succeed without bloodshed – I hope so – but I know that this is not the end of history and that we must try to put down transnational tyranny before it puts us down. Like our ancestors, we must move from subjecthood to citizenship, from being victims to being actors in our own destiny.

Shifts in the balance of power require assessing one's *numbers*, *forces* and capacity for making *alliances*. The numbers are there – geographically separated and politically divided, but there. The Working Party is quite correct from its own standpoint in stating that separateness and division must be encouraged. Although 'we' are generally only too happy to comply, perhaps they can be surmounted. The forces should be sufficient as well if only because of the great numbers of social sectors which stand to lose from arbitrary corporate power and transnational tyranny. The alliances are trickier because they must be trans-generational, trans-sectoral, trans-boundary and sometimes trans-political, making for the strangest of bedfellows.

In the USA, it took the right and left joining forces to defeat the President's 'fast-track' authority (to sign free trade agreements into law with no amendments from Congress). As a friend of mine said when watching two French agricultural confederations squabble over some relatively minor matter, 'Right-wing peasants, left-wing peasants, who cares? There aren't going to *be* any peasants!' So they had better get together on essentials but it's not a natural reflex for them or for other groups used to splitting along time-worn and time-honoured lines.

Sometimes the allies, in a truly bizarre twist, may even be … transnationals. The insurance industry, for example, is exceedingly worried about global warming because it increases the frequency of tropical storms. One needn't agree on everything to work together on something, although I draw the line at major predators and polluters. Let them earn their stripes somewhere else, through their own efforts before using popular movements as fig leaves.

In spite of the obstacles, the positive side is that everyone can – should – become involved because the task of all tasks is to reweave the social fabric that neo-liberalism is rending. It's no good saying, 'But what can *I* do?' I can't do anything, I'm only …' Fill in the blank. We are all 'only …' Each one can become a thread of the warp or the weft. Every bridge built, every channel dug, every pathway worn goes somewhere and helps to recreate the human landscape.

Myriad activities are taking place at the local level as people fight here a toxic waste dump, there an intrusive, unnecessary highway, elsewhere a plant closing. Some of these initiatives can be linked, for example, through the promising Sustainable and Self-Reliant Communities Movement. The more economic activities that can be recaptured and withdrawn from the transnational orbit, the better.

Dozens of towns of different sizes are already experimenting with locally held joint stock companies to supply goods and services satisfying local needs; countryside-to-town food co-ops directly linking farmers and consumers are being set up, community banks are viable, Local Exchange Trading Systems (LETS) are flourishing, dozens of alternative currencies are already in circulation.[11]

People fighting for the well-being of their families and their communities do not necessarily think of themselves as 'activists' or 'environmentalists'. Neither did their predecessors in the nineteenth century when they fought against children working in the mines, adulterated food and milk or an end to the twelve-hour day and demanded the right to rest on Sundays. All such struggles concern at base the integrity of the human body, whether the target is an incinerator in South Central Los Angeles, smog in post-war London or rats in Brazilian slums. Sometimes those who do call themselves environmentalists should think much more about the human body, shape their issues in order to defend it and frame their arguments in terms that everyone can understand.

Some maintain that changing the scale and 'going local' are enough. I disagree, however much I encourage these initiatives. Unless we can make sure that the state retains its prerogatives, I can't see who will stand between the person on the ground and transnational tyranny. Without the state – though not necessarily the one we have now – it will soon be McSchools, McHealth and McTransport.

Strengthening local and national democracy, creating dissident, parallel economies are paramount and something in which everyone can participate. The toughest task will still be to create alternative globalisation, which some organisations are beginning to call 'cooperative globalisation'. For them, the concept means not a return or an escape to the local but as an effort to rebuild the global economy from the bottom up, on the basis of healthier, more equitable societies.

There are literally thousands, millions of jobs available in the 'social economy' or 'third sector' between public and private but so far most governments can't see them because they exist chiefly in the form of unmet needs. Brazilian workers, for example, are inventing the 'socio-economy' or 'public non-state sector' based on cooperatives with a wide range of forms of ownership and management which can cooperate and trade *with each othe*r to avoid dog-eat-dog competitive market relations altogether. They have already linked with Uruguayan and Spanish workers' cooperatives organised along similar lines.

The Fair Trade movement is also gaining ground and members. Best known for 'alternative' tea and coffee supplied to the North by Southern workers' co-ops, it is now moving well beyond this first stage to supply supermarkets and collectives (municipalities, universities and the like). In Britain, Christian Aid, using customer pressure, is encouraging supermarkets to take responsibility for the conditions under which the items on their shelves are produced in the South. University students and professors are asking their canteens to serve organic food grown by local producers and to supply fair-trade beverages. If you join with others, you can use your consumption to promote justice.

Trade unions are also beginning to organise transnationally. When workers run in the race to the bottom, everyone loses. If they could achieve company-wide unions across the globe, they could successfully challenge corporate power. The point is to bring wages and working conditions worldwide up to decent levels, not fight one another for crumbs; to establish floors, not ceilings.

A French humorist once wrote, 'When it's money you're after, look for it where it is most abundant, among the poor.' Governments now do this more than ever because the poor are rooted, stationary, 'slow'; whereas the big money is nomadic and travels at the speed of bytes. Stationary money (of local businesses, professionals, wage and salary earners) will be taxed to the limit for the simple reason that it can be got at.

The only way to pay for everything that needs doing – eradicating hunger, environmental renewal, health and education for all – is to go after the money where it really is, among the TNCs and on the financial markets. Many proposals for the so-called 'Tobin Tax' on international financial transactions (FOREX) have been floated. Coupled with a trifling purchase/sales tax on stocks, bonds, options, and their fancy derivative cousins could put money in the coffers of the UN and its agencies faster than they could spend it.

But to earn the privilege of spending it, those agencies too would have to become responsible and accountable to someone besides transnationals and their own handpicked boards of governors. The UN and the TNCs now meet in cosy settings like the Geneva Business Dialogue (a joint venture of the International Chamber of Commerce and the UN), the Transatlantic Business Dialogue (heads of TNCs and top national and international officeholders) in multiple 'consensus-building' exercises. If international bureaucracies want to escape charges of favouritism, they should insist that other groups also be invited in sufficient numbers to make sure that alternative voices are heard.

If international taxation is instituted, citizen organisations should have a say in how the money is spent, specific proportions could be allocated to co-ops and other decentralised enterprises and to democratically elected governments of poor countries making efforts to supply health and education to their people. Such taxes will not happen by magic but could be instituted if enough governments are told loudly and clearly by enough citizens that they want the tax burden shared.

One could start by financing a huge international Keynesian environmental conversion and clean-up programme. Ecological taxation is the only longer-term solution to environmental destruction. The old principle is applicable internationally: tax what you want less of, de-tax what you want more of. De-tax employment and revenue, tax pollution and waste in order to push business on to the right environmental track.

Does all this mean that focusing on world population is unimportant? No, population is a genuine, deeply troubling issue. But unless one wants the Lugano Solution, one must take seriously the Report's chapter on prevention in which several avenues are charted. The most effective is to supply education and choice for women, impossible under current structural adjustment austerity programmes.

Some basic rules apply whatever the path of action chosen: first, identify the goal and the obstacles which stand in the way of reaching the goal. Seek to organise as many stakeholders as possible to achieve it. Then remember the wisdom of the ancient Chinese strategist Sun Tzu: do not do what you would most like to do. Do what your adversary would least like you to do. Act transnationally whenever possible: the threat is transnational, so must be the riposte. Internet connections are now so simple that we too can be 'fast people'.

People organised in transnational alliances can go a long way to shaping the future but I also believe that events will conspire to overturn strategies like those proposed by *The Lugano Report*. I hasten to temper this apparent optimism by pointing out that the circumstances are likely to be quite dire and I wish they could be avoided. This Annexe is about alternatives so I shall not describe my fears in detail; however, I want to be on record on the subject of economic/financial meltdown, or what the Working Party calls a 'global accident' and social upheaval on a grand scale. Houses of cards tend to collapse and the 'self-regulating' market, as Karl Polanyi saw decades ago, will tear society apart.[12]

Finally, if further moral grounds are thought to be needed for opposing transnational tyranny, one may turn to John Rawls's *Theory of Justice*.[13] Before you choose the basic principles that should govern it, imagine society from the point of view of someone who is ignorant of his or her own place in it; of the talents and opportunities with which he or she will be gifted in life. You would then choose a world in which 'social and economic inequalities [are] arranged so that they are to the greatest benefit of the least advantaged'. You would surely not choose a world subject to the logic of *The Lugano Report*. There is a choice.

Afterword to *The Lugano Report*

It's no secret: I wrote *The Lugano Report* myself from start to finish. To explain why I did so, however, requires a brief account of my work to date. Since the mid-1970s when I began researching my first book, *How the Other Half Dies,*[1] I have always sought to understand and to describe how power is deployed. From this vantage point, I have dealt with such subjects as world hunger and Third World poverty, the impact of southern hemisphere debt, North–South relations, transnational corporations and institutions like the World Bank. Many people have consequently assumed that I am either a development expert, an economist, or both.

In fact I am neither. I have never lived or worked in a developing country and, aside from a long-ago 101 course, have never formally studied economics. My three university degrees were acquired at ten-year intervals. The first was a 'double major' in French and government from Smith College in the United States; the second a 'Licence ès Philosophie' from the Sorbonne. My doctoral dissertation concerned the forcible transfer of the US food system to the rest of the world, consummating a smorgasbord of seminars in and around the Ecole des Hautes Etudes en Sciences Sociales. It was so trans-disciplinary that the proper authorities finally stuffed it into the Sorbonne category of 'North American Studies: Option Political Science'.[2]

Perhaps the single common thread running through this mélange is my penchant for asking in any given circumstances who is in control and how they use their power, which groups get the benefits and which pay the costs. Once I feel I've more or less answered those questions, I tend rightly or wrongly to move on instead of ploughing the same furrow season after season.

So it happened that from the mid-1990s, after Fabrizio Sabelli and I had finished *Faith and Credit: The World Bank's Secular Empire,*[3] I was looking for a fresh, new patch. Environmental questions increasingly preoccupied me, partly thanks to serving six years on the Greenpeace International Board. Reminders of ecological predation and destruction flooded my computer daily via the 'greenlink'.

Then in early 1995, a month or so after the Mexican financial meltdown, I wrote a proposal-cum-introduction for a book to be called *Perfect Crimes*. It would set out to show why other crises, in other 'emerging markets', would necessarily follow, causing enormous human suffering for those who had not sown the financial landmines but were invariably hit by the shrapnel when they exploded. The hypothesis was correct, as Russia and Asia have since proved, but such a book needed a substantial travel budget and I couldn't raise the money. So I wrote shorter pieces and continued to observe the ongoing offensive against the earth and the substitution of market 'law' for the social contract. These seemed to me the most salient features of globalisation.

Concerning the ravages of what is known as Thatcherism in Britain, Reaganism in the United States and neo-liberalism nearly everywhere else, I had to wonder how they got away with it. How was it possible to up-end Robin Hood, to take systematically from the poor to give to the rich or, in more theoretical terms, to remunerate capital to the detriment of labour? Any number of studies made crystal clear the fact that these transfers were taking place on a huge and global scale, both within and between countries.[4]

Thus the top 1 per cent of American families doubled their incomes in the Reagan years while 80 per cent of ordinary families lost. The further down the scale they were, the more they lost proportionally. The story was approximately the same in Britain. Internationally speaking, income disparities between the top and bottom fifths of humanity had doubled in three decades. Third World debt was an ingenious mechanism for shifting wealth from Southern poor to Southern elites and thence northwards, while entrenching political and economic control in the World Bank and the IMF. Examples were legion.

At Transnational Institute Fellows' Meetings, we spoke routinely of the 'Global North' – made up of the international elites and increasingly anxious middle classes – and the 'Global South' – those unneeded and unwanted by world markets wherever they lived – and of the population of the planet as 'one-thirds in, two-thirds out'.[5]

The world seemed set on such a destructive course financially, socially and ecologically that like many others I was seriously alarmed. I still am, but my point is that dealing with the inter-related aspects of economic globalisation and its dire human and planetary consequences seemed to call for something stronger than another book of explanation and criticism.

What that 'something' might be was still far from clear. But I began trying to see these same phenomena from the point of view of those in charge, those who profit most from existing arrangements. They may be ruthless, they may lack all compassion for the 'losers' of their system, but they are by no means stupid. Surely they too must hear alarm bells ringing and see warning lights flashing. They *had* to be worried.

And they were! Alan Greenspan was worried about irrational market exuberance, George Soros was worried about the excesses of capitalism, the chief economist of the World Bank was worried about the impact and severity of structural adjustment programmes in poor countries, the director of global economics at Morgan Stanley was worried about the coming 'raw power struggle between capital and labour' and lots of people were worried about social polarisation and environmental collapse. No one, however, seemed to be pulling all this together, at least not in public.

If *I* were among those in charge, I thought, I would make damn sure it got pulled together and would be prepared to pay handsomely for a no-holds-barred assessment of the system's health and resilience, if only because my future power and profits depended upon them. If that diagnosis revealed grave dangers in store for me and others like me, I would also want a prescription which could help me to buck the trends and bend the future.

Slowly the idea for *The Lugano Report* took shape. One would have to keep constantly in mind the perspective of the masters of the universe. I asked myself how one or two prominent, though informal, groups (which I shall not name so as not to invite legal action) might proceed.

They would commission a high-powered study group entirely composed of North American and European men, recruited from different disciplines. The group's members would be what Americans call 'policy intellectuals', the kind who switch effortlessly from academia to government and back, running prestigious university centres and acting as highly placed advisers. They would carry weight in their respective fields but they would not be household names. Working under conditions of strict secrecy, meeting in neutral territory, keeping their identities unknown, possibly even to each other, they would communicate between meetings through dedicated e-mail, using pseudonyms. And, of course, they would be more than generously compensated for their time. Their mandate would be to examine the state of the world system and report to the Commissioners on how best to keep it ticking over so that it could continue to advance their aims.

For quite a while, I wanted to see if I could make the group's 'Report' pass as genuine (though I always intended to confess authorship in the end). Eventually, for reasons too boring to explain, I gave up on the idea of the credible hoax, but not before I had written a fictional foreword explaining how I came to be in possession of *The Lugano Report*. In this fantasy, I gave my protagonists wild-flower pseudonyms as an *aide-mémoire* for the disciplines involved. They were anthropologist Asphodel, biologist Burdock, demographer Dill, economist Edelweiss, philosopher Foxglove, historian Hawkweed, political scientist Pennycress, sociologist Cinquefoil and scientist-ecologist Snowbell. And so they have remained in their 'Letter of Transmittal'. The tenth member of the group, called Gentian, was master of ceremonies, organiser and general factotum. In my fiction, he had personally contacted each member of the group on behalf of sponsors who preferred not to declare their individual or collective identities but who, he intimated, were highly placed, important personages.

Thus the Working Party never knew exactly whom they were working for, but their material rewards dampened any residual curiosity or misgivings. Their meetings took place in a large and comfortable house in a town in 'neutral', i.e. Swiss, territory, at once charming, discreet and rich. Lugano sprang readily to mind.

So much for the genesis and the format of *The Lugano Report*. I could not imagine one that could better allow me to say what I felt needed saying and to weave apparently disparate strands into a coherent pattern. The group's premises and its mandate had to be pushed to their logical conclusions.

As far as I know, the empirical and theoretical literature has never drawn these conclusions although they seem to me to be staring us in the face. Our present system is a universal machine for ravaging the environment and for producing losers that no one has a clue what to do with.

I hope readers are chilled by *The Lugano Report*, but I want to stress that it is not sensationalist. Nor is it a 'satire', some sort of millennial *Modest Proposal*. The content is entirely based on fat dossiers of factual material, just like my other books. It is less densely footnoted than the others because I thought that Working Party members would consider their own authority sufficient, but they always have solid evidence for saying what they say. Should readers doubt this, they are invited to complain and I will dig out the required reference(s) from one of my several boxes of supporting documents.

In other words, *The Lugano Report* is as accurate, sober and detached an assessment as serious research could make it. It is not a work of science fiction or any other kind of fiction. Aside from the basic conceit, nothing is made up and I would not be in the least surprised to learn that a similar document has actually been produced by a real-life Working Party.

One or two friends have suggested that I should make compellingly clear which parts of the 'Report' actually reflect my own ideas and which do not; they say this kindly, implying that I have not sufficiently covered, not to put too fine a point on it, my backside.

At the risk of truly tiresome repetition of matters that I feel have been already adequately dealt with here and in the Annexe, I stress that I did my best to make the Lugano conclusions flow from the Working Party's premises and its desired outcomes for the world economy. It does not follow that I accept the premises (except for the ecological ones), much less the outcomes, and even less the methods. I also believe the world is headed their way if radical reordering within and between nations is not undertaken forthwith. This book is intended to afflict the comfortable without, alas, providing much comfort to the afflicted. But these are not pretty times and the stakes are high.

Some specific examples:

- Perhaps I will have interesting arguments with people who defend 'identity politics' (see Part Two, Chapter 2, 'Pillars') with which I have little patience because of their myriad divide-and-rule advantages.

- Left-leaning foundations have in my view shown stupidity bordering on the criminal in not defending – that is, putting money into – progressive ideas. The Working Party understands the importance of creating and using ideology.[6]

- Releasing untold numbers of genetically modified organisms into the environment seems to me suicidal – and thus suited to the Lugano goals in the South.

And so on. Sometimes I'm highlighting the ruthlessness of the Right, sometimes criticising what I see as the blindness or shibboleths of the Left. That should alienate pretty much everyone, and if not, these mandatory, I'm told, paragraphs insulting the reader's intelligence should do the trick.

A final word of acknowledgement: Roger van Zwanenberg and Robert Webb at Pluto have placed their considerable energies and professionalism in the service of this book and I am greatly in their debt. As to the help with the content, I was familiar with much of the terrain covered in the 'Report' before I started and knew on the whole where to go for information in areas where I was less at ease. Many people lent me a hand; naming them might not always be to their advantage. My gratitude to three of them, however, cannot go unrecorded: Alex Brenner for his multilingual, painstaking and cheerful research assistance; Fabrizio Sabelli for his intellectual rigour, sustaining friendship and critical comments always tempered with kindness; Charles-Henry George for reading every line and keeping my spirits up with his material and moral support throughout. Nobody should have to live with a writer: CHG somehow does, with patience and panache.

Notes

Part 1

Chapter 1.1 Dangers

1. The scientific name of the system under discussion is 'capitalism'. However, since the writings of Karl Marx, the term has acquired unnecessarily negative connotations in some quarters. Having established this, we will from now on generally use 'free-market' or 'market' economy instead of 'capitalism'. Our perspective is that of 'liberalism' in its classic sense; somewhat confusingly, in North America, 'liberals' stand to the left of centre and defend the welfare state. The terms 'neo-liberal' or 'neo-conservative' would also be applicable to our analysis.
2. *The Entropy Law and the Economic Process*, Harvard University Press, Cambridge, Mass., 1971.
3. 'The entropy of a closed system increases with time' or 'heat cannot be transferred by any continuous, self-sustaining process from a colder to a hotter body'.
4. This part of our Report had been completed before the Korean and Indonesian debacles of November–December 1997.

Chapter 1.2 Control

1. See Per Bak and Kan Chen, 'Self-Organised Criticality', *Scientific American*, January 1991, pp. 46–53; also Per Bak, *How Nature Works*, Copernicus/Springer Verlag, 1996.
2. The Governors of the G-10 Central Banks will finally institute a reporting system, effective in June 1998, for foreign exchange, interest rate, equity and commodity-based derivative instruments which are multi-trillion dollar markets. Bank for International Settlements, *International Banking and Financial Market Developments*, Basle, May 1997.
3. In the early 1980s, the average American family needed 18 weeks' salary to purchase an average car; by the mid-1990s, the figure had grown to 28 weeks of salary. This information figures in William Greider's book, *One World Ready or Not*, Simon and Schuster, New

York, 1997. We find Greider utterly mistaken in many respects, but his points concerning over-capacity and possible deflation are well taken.

Chapter 1.3   Impact

1. Initially by Professor Paul Ehrlich (who prefers A for Affluence to C for Consumption, so his formula is I=PAT): P. Erlich and J. Holdren, 'Impact of Population Growth', *Science*; Vol. 171 (1971), pp. 1212–17; subsequently used by many other scholars in various guises.
2. Comparisons are based on the Purchasing Power Parity (PPP) methodology which is more reliable, or at least less faulty, than comparing consumption expenditures in local currencies with an exchange rate conversion.
3. Nor can one discount present and potential costs of nuclear energy associated with long-term storage, safety, military security and terrorism.
4. Figures calculated from United Nations Population Division estimates which are officially 'state of the art'. Other, less official sources put the net population increase in the closing years of the twentieth century at 90 to 100 million a year.
5. The 'ecological footprint' method has been pioneered by Professor William Rees at the University of British Columbia, Vancouver: see William Rees and Mathias Wackernagel, *Our Ecological Footprint*, New Society Publishers, Philadelphia and Gabriola Island, BC, Canada, 1996.
6. Garrett Hardin, 'The Tragedy of the Commons', *Science*, Vol. 162, 13 December 1968, pp. 1243–8.
7. Karl Marx, *The German Ideology* (Materialist Theory, Dominant Classes and Ideas).

Chapter 1.4   Conclusions

1. Plato, *The Republic*, 459b *et seq*.
2. Aristotle, *The Politics*, Book II, Chapter VII.
3. Samuel P. Huntington, *The Clash of Civilisations and the Remaking of World Order*, Simon and Schuster, New York, 1996, especially Chapter 8.

Part 2

Chapter 2.1 Goals

1. Saint Augustine, quoted in Thomas Aquinas, *Summa Theologica*, question 2, article 3.
2. Arne Naess and George Sessions, *The Deep Ecology Platform*, 1985, published as a broadsheet.
3. Niccolò Machiavelli, *The Prince* (1513), Chapter V.
4. For the mathematically inclined, the curve is a parabola $y = ax^2 + bx + c$ such that $y = -0.009x^2 + 0.08x + 6$.

Chapter 2.2 Pillars

1. Tertullian (AD 150–222?), *On the Soul*, cited by Garrett Hardin, *Living Within Limits*, Oxford University Press, New York and Oxford, 1993, pp. 105–6 (our emphasis).
2. The five largest global media conglomerates are Time Warner ($25 billion sales), Disney ($24 billion), Bertelsmann ($15 billion), Viacom ($13 billion) and News Corporation (Murdoch, $10 billion). Their assets include newspapers, magazines, films, television, video, CD-Roms, books, and so on.
3. See Matt Ridley, *The Origins of Virtue*, Penguin, Harmondsworth, 1996, particularly Chapters 3 and 4.

Chapter 2.3 Scourges

1. Colin McEvedy and Richard Jones, *Atlas of World Population History*, Penguin, Harmondsworth, 1980, p. 21.
2. Michel Foucault, 'Cours du 17 mars 1976' (transcription of the lesson pronounced by Foucault in his course at the Collège de France), in *Il Faut Défendre la Société*, Gallimard-Seuil, Paris, 1997, especially pp. 218ff.
3. Emily Martin, *Flexible Bodies: Tracking Immunity in American Culture from the Days of Polio to the Age of AIDS*, Beacon Press, Boston, 1994. Ms Martin is Professor of Anthropology at Princeton University and participated herself in this training course which was organised for 22,000 employees of a 'Fortune 500' corporation.
4. Peace Research Institute of Oslo (PRIO), *Causes and Dynamics of Conflict Escalation*, Report on a Research Project, June 1997; also Dan Smith (with PRIO), *The State of War and Peace Atlas*, Penguin, New York and Harmondsworth, 1997.

5. For further information, see Michael T. Klare, 'The arms trade in the 1990s: Changing patterns, rising dangers', *Third World Quarterly*, Vol. 17, No. 5, pp. 857–74, 1996; R.T. Naylor, 'Loose cannons: Covert commerce and underground finance in the modern arms black market', *Crime, Law and Social Change*, 22, pp. 1–57, 1995, Kluwer Academic Publishers; William W. Keller, *Arm in Arm: the Political Economy of the Global Arms Trade*, Basic Books, New York, 1995.

6. Martin van Creveld, *The Transformation of War*, New York, The Free Press, New York,1991, p. 197.

7. Passages in quote marks are from several articles by Major Ralph Peters, responsible for future warfare, Office of the Deputy Chief of Staff for Intelligence of the United States Army. These articles all appeared in *Parameters*, the US Army War College Quarterly, between 1995 and 1997.

8. Major Ralph Peters, 'Constant Conflict', *Parameters*, Summer 1997, pp. 4–14.

9. 'Food security' is defined as 'Access by all people at all times to enough food for an active and healthy life' (World Bank); 'Food security means that food is available at all times, that all persons have means of access to it, that it is nutritionally adequate in terms of quantity, quality and variety, and that it is acceptable within the given culture' (FAO).

10. This catch-all term refers to short-straw, high-yielding varieties of wheat and rice and the package of industrial inputs (fertilisers, pesticides and irrigation systems) needed to cultivate them. Initially financed by the Rockefeller and Ford Foundations, they were introduced in the 1960s and 1970s by US-affiliated researchers working in politically sensitive, food-deficit areas, particularly India, Mexico and the Philippines.

11. An adult consuming less than 2,700 calories a day is not absolutely malnourished but according to most nutritional estimates will still be subject to serious illness and/or deficiencies. Above 2,700 calories, one can live a 'normal' life; heavy manual work requires up to 4,500 calories a day.

12. Lester Brown, *Who Will Feed China? Wake-up call for a small planet*, Earthscan Publications, London,1996.

13. Justin Yifu Lin, Jikun Huang and Scott Rozelle, 'China's Food Economy: Past Performance and Future Trends', in *China in the 21st Century*, OECD, Paris, 1996, Chapter 8.

14. J.L. Fox citing Professor Fred Gould in 'Bt cotton infestations renew resistance concerns', *Nature Biotechnology*, 14 September 1996, p. 1070.

15. J.E. Meade, 'Population Explosion, the Standard of Living and Social Conflict', Presidential Address to the Royal Economic Society, 30 June 1966, in *The Economic Journal*, Cambridge, Vol. 77, No. 306, June 1967, pp. 233–55.
16. This burden is measured in terms of DALYs or Disability Adjusted Life Years, a complex methodology measuring years of life lost to premature death and years lived with a disability of specified severity and duration.
17. World Bank, *World Development Report 1993: Investing in Health*, p. 9, our emphasis.
18. Colonel C. William Fox, Jr, MD (who commanded the MEDFLAG operations), 'Phantom Warriors: Disease as a Threat to US National Security', *Parameters*, Winter 1997–98, pp. 121–36.
19. This quote and some subsequent information in Laurie Garrett, 'The Post-Antibiotic Era', *Foreign Affairs*, January–February 1996, pp. 66–79.
20. Howard S. Gold, MD and Robert C. Moellering, Jr, MD, 'Antimicrobial-Drug Resistance', *The New England Journal of Medicine*, Vol. 335, No. 19, 7 November 1996, pp. 1445–53.
21. Cited in PANOS, *WorldAIDS*, London and Washington DC, No. 38, March 1995.

Chapter 2.4 Prevention

1. These 'countries' were invented by Professor J.E. Meade in 'Population Explosion, the Standard of Living and Social Conflict', Presidential Address to the Royal Economic Society, 30 June 1966, *The Economic Journal*, 77 (1967), pp. 233–55. We have added political variables to his economic ones to account more fully for the different demographic outcomes.
2. The World Health Organisation, the UN Population Fund, and others, speak of 'contraception', 'abortion', 'sterilisation' separately: we prefer to use 'Reproductive Inhibitors' or RI because the term describes more accurately and succinctly the goal aspired to here.
3. United Nations Population Fund, *The State of World Population 1997*, New York, pp. 22–3.
4. Stories based on information in *Creating Common Ground in Asia: women's perspectives on the selection and introduction of fertility regulation technologies*, WHO Human Reproduction Programme, 1994.
5. See Judith Richter, *Vaccination Against Pregnancy: Miracle or Menace?*, Zed Books, London, 1996.
6. Snehalata Vishwanath, 'May I Have Some More Milk Pills, Please?', *Reproductive Health Matters*, London, No. 3, May 1994.

Chapter 2.5 Puzzles

1. Kent E. Calder (Senior Adviser to the US State Department for East Asian and Pacific Affairs), *Asia's Deadly Triangle: how arms, energy and growth threaten to destabilize Asia-Pacific*, Nicholas Brealey Publishing, London, 1997.

2. Mark Hertsgaard, 'Our Real China Problem', *The Atlantic Monthly*, November 1997 and *Earth Odyssey: Around the World in Search of Our Environmental Future*, Broadway Books, Little Brown, New York and London, forthcoming. More devastating floods, often worsened by deforestation, can also be expected.

3. *Chinese Statistical Yearbook 1996* and research by the Hong Kong Christian Industrial Committee, Kowloon, in their bulletin *Change*, various issues, 1997.

4. See details of military support in the paper by two retired US army colonels with deep knowledge of this 'war': William W. Mendel and Murl D. Munger, 'The Drug Threat: Getting Priorities Straight', *Parameters* (US Army War College Quarterly), Summer 1997.

5. Lieutenant-Commander Wayne G. Shear, 'The Drug War, Applying the Lessons of Vietnam', *Naval War College Review*, Summer 1994, p. 120; cited in Peter Zirnite, *Relectant Recruits: the US Military and the War on Drugs*, Washington Office on Latin America, August 1997, p. 36.

Annexe

1. Albert J. Dunlap with Bob Andelman, Times Books, New York, 1996.

2. Lovers of poetic justice will be pleased to learn that Mr Dunlap was himself downsized in 1998.

3. United Nations, *World Investment Report 1996*, pp.123–125 provides a fuller explanation.

4. For further information, ITGLWF Federation, rue Joseph Stevens 8, 1000 Brussels, Belgium, fax (32–2) 511 0904.

5. *Coast Hotel Co.* v. *Parrish*, 1937.

6. For a useful book on these topics by an honest, self-designated 'neo-classical economist', see Dani Rodrik, *Has Globalization Gone Too Far?*, Institute for International Economics, Washington, DC 1997. Rodrik says it hasn't, 'Not if policy makers act wisely and imaginatively.' A large 'if' from an economist whose politics are naive at best, but here's hoping.

7. See Doug Henwood, *Wall Street*, Verso, New York and London, 1998; also Professor Paul H. Dembinski (University of Fribourg), in

various publications of the Financial Monitoring Centre in Geneva.

8. Garrett Hardin, 'The Tragedy of the Commons', *Science* 162 (1968), pp. 1243–48

9. I am prepared to give a cash award called the Qualm Prize to anyone who discovers anything remotely resembling a qualm emerging from the IMF. (Definition of 'qualm' in the *OED*: 'Momentary faint or sick feeling, queasiness, misgiving, sinking of heart, scruple of conscience, doubt of one's own rectitude in some matter.' Entries on any or all of these grounds acceptable.)

10. See John McMurtry, *The Cancer Stage of Capitalism*, Pluto Press, London, 1999.

11. Check http://www.ips.org/ifps; also Michael Shuman, *Going Local: Creating Self-Reliant Communities in a Global Age*, The Free Press, New York, forthcoming.

12. In *The Great Transformation*, 1962.

14. Beacon Press, Boston, 1957 [first published by Rinehart and Co., 1944].

Afterword

1. Penguin, Harmondsworth, 1976

2. Published as *Les Stratèges de la Faim*, Editions Grounauer, Geneva, 1981.

3. Penguin, Harmondsworth, 1994.

4. For a good summary, see UNCTAD, *Trade and Development Report 1997*, Chapter 3.

5. Concepts developed particularly by John Cavanagh and Walden Bello, with input from other TNI colleagues.

6. See Susan George, 'How to Win the War of Ideas: Lessons from the Gramscian Right', *Dissent*, Summer 1997.

Index

Index compiled by Sue Carlton